THE THEORY OF SWEETENED BAKERY FOODS

DR ANSHUMALI PANDEY

Contents

Contents

Preface

In my previous books **"Bakery Ingredients and Tools"** and **"Bread and Rolls"** you have learned about the basic ingredients and their role in baking, and about the Yeast related baking part of Breads and Rolls.

Now in this book **"The Theory of Sweetened Bakery Foods"** we will be learning about making various types of Sweetened bread and Pastries and Cakes.

The language used in this book is simple without any pictorial illustration to keep the cost low and affordable to all. This book is a complete handbook for anybody to even start a small bakery. This book will help students by giving them information in simple story telling style.

My dear friend, the author of the book (me) is a practicing professional from the fields of Hospitality and Tourism and has an experience of over 26 years.

Happy Baking and healthy eating!!!

Dr Anshumali Pandey

Prologue

Book 1 of 3 in Bakery

Book 2 of 3 in Bakery

Please refer the first two books as well if possible, to get a continuity to this current book, which you are holding infront of you. Best wishes.

CHAPTER ONE

INTRODUCTION

Dough is a thick, malleable, sometimes elastic paste made out of any grains, leguminous or chestnut crops. Dough is typically made by mixing flour with a small amount of water and/or other liquid, and sometimes includes yeast or other leavening agents as well as other ingredients such as various fats or flavorings.

The process of making and shaping dough is a precursor to making a wide variety of foodstuffs, particularly breads and bread –based items, but also including biscuits, cakes, cookies, dumplings, flatbreads, noodles, pasta, pastry, pizza, piecrusts, and similar items. Doughs are made from a wide variety of flours, commonly wheat but also flours made from maize, rice, rye, legumes, almonds, and other cereals and crops used around the world.

Words are complicated. There's so many of them, and some of them sound the same but are spelled differently, and mean different things. Similar is the case of Pastry where this word becomes enormously confusing. A pastry chef in a restaurant is in charge of pretty much anything sweet or baked, which can include but not be limited to: breads, cakes, pie, ice cream, candies, mousses, muffins, sweet breads, puddings, cookies, laminated dough pastries, entremets, and both chocolate and sugar work. But if you look up the word pastry in a dictionary it seems to pretty much indicate a dough paste made with a solid fat that is rolled, like a pie crust or puff pastry, where the word pastry is right in the name to either eliminate confusion or add to it, depending on your mood.

So if a pastry chef makes cake, does that make cake pastry? And if we postulate such a theory, are we suddenly in the middle of some high school logic exam question? If all cake is baked and all baked goods are pastry then all cake is pastry. But if all pastry is not cake, then what is it?

Pastry is dough of flour, water and shortening that may be savory or sweetened. Sweetened pastries are often described as bakers' confectionery. The word "pastries" suggests many kinds of baked products made from ingredients such as flour, sugar, milk, butter, shortening, baking powder, and eggs. Small tarts and other sweet baked products are called pastries. The French word patisserie is also used in English (with or without the accent) for the same foods. Common pastry dishes include pies, tarts, quiches and pasties. Pastry can also refer to the pastry dough from which such baked products are made. Pastry dough is rolled out thinly and used as a base for baked products.

Pastry is differentiated from bread by having a higher fat content, which contributes to a flaky or crumbly texture. A good pastry is light and airy and fatty, but firm enough to support the weight of the filling.

Various types of pastries are used in the preparation of sweet and savory dishes in the bakery and confectionery. These include: Short crust pastry, Flaky pastry, Puff pastry, Danish pastry, Choux pastry, Rough puff pastry, and Hot water pastry.

CHAPTER TWO

RICH DOUGH

Basic sweet yeast dough is enriched dough, also known as rich dough. This means that the dough is made with fat, sugar, and sometimes eggs, as opposed to lean doughs that do not have any fat present. The addition of fat to yeast dough creates bread that tends to have a softer crust and less chewy crumb and is more flavorful in general. Danish, croissant, cinnamon roll or a Jewish challah, Baba, Hot cross buns, Brioche are some of the sweet yeast dough products.

Common recipes that create rich dough: Adding in different amounts and ingredients, like eggs and butter, can turn rich dough into a variety of breads: Add oil and you have challah or cinnamon roll; add butter and swap the water for milk, and you are on your way to glorious brioche; add a touch more sugar and a sweet filling or glaze and you've got sticky buns or sugary breakfast rolls; fold in butter results in laminated dough for making different products. Sometimes using the same base dough and simply filling or shaping it differently can result in an entirely different product. The basic sweet yeast dough recipe uses the Modified Straight Dough Method, which is a method for mixing rich yeast dough.

This method ensures even distribution of the fat and sugar present in the dough.Generally sweet yeast doughs take longer time to ferment and rise, this is because of the following reasons:

Sugar: Whereas lean doughs only have at most 5 percent sugar, rich doughs can have up to 10 percent. The hydroscopic nature of sugar attracts the moisture making the gluten harder for the yeast to hydrate. This tussle of attracting of water by the sugar and the yeast results in delayed fermentation of the dough.

Salt: Salt is important for developing flavor and taste. It helps in strengthening the gluten and hinders the growth of yeast, thus regulates the yeast's activity, making sure it does not go overboard and expand uncontrollably. Too much salt, however, will slow down fermentation.

Fat: The extra fat (butter, oil, and eggs) that makes rich dough regulated the reproduction of yeast and also has less capability of holding the air pockets in the dough.

However, no dough the process of fermentation of the dough is very slow, but the final product is more flavorful, soft and of supple texture.

Recipe of basic sweet yeast dough Ingredients
—

- Whole milk – 1 cup
- Sugar– 5 tbsp, divided
- Active dry yeast – 1 tsp
- Large eggs, room temperature – 2 nos
- Unbleached all –purpose flour – 1 cup
- Salt –1 tsp

- unsalted solid butter, (cut into 1 –inch pieces, room temperature) – ½ cup
- Melted butter – ½ tbsp

Method –

- Heat milk in a small saucepan over medium heat.
- Transfer milk to a 2 –cup measuring cup; stir in 1 tbsp. sugar. Sprinkle yeast over milk and whisk to blend. Let sit until yeast is foamy, about 5 minutes.
- Add eggs and whisk until smooth.
- Combine remaining 4 tbsp. sugar, flour and salt in the bowl , add the flavour if any in very small quantity.
- Add milk mixture. Stir in cut and fold method, add ½cup room –temperature butter, 1 piece at a time, blending well between additions. Mix for 1 minute and then knead at medium –high speed until dough is soft and silky, about 5 – 10 minutes.
- Brush a medium bowl with some melted butter; place dough in bowl. Brush top of dough with remaining melted butter; cover with plastic wrap. Can be made 1 day ahead. Cover with plastic; chill.
- Let dough rise in a warm, moisture –free area until doubled in size, 1–1 ½ hours (or 2–2 ½ hours if dough has been refrigerated).
- Use it as required with baking temperature of the products – 190⁰C.

DANISH PASTRY

A Danish pastry, sometimes also known as just Danish, is a multilayered, laminated sweet pastry in the viennoiserie tradition. This pastry type is named Danish because it originates from Denmark. The concept was brought to Denmark by Austrian bakers, and has since developed into a Danish specialty. Like other Viennoiserie pastries, such as croissants, it is a variant of puff pastry made of laminated yeast –leavened dough that creates a layered texture. It consists out of yeast –leavened dough and a type of fat; mostly butter or margarine. The fat can be included in the dough or it can be attached into the dough by laminating. The dough is rolled out thinly, then folded with a layer of butter to form multiple layers. Multilayered dough (dough –fat –dough) in most cases builds up in between 16 to 36 layers. Butter is the traditional fat used in Danish pastry, but in industrial production, less expensive fats are often used, such as hydrogenated fat called margarine. In Danish, Norwegian, and Swedish, the term for Danish pastry is wienerbrød (or wienerbröd), meaning "Viennese bread".

In the United Kingdom, various ingredients such as jam, custard, apricots, cherries, raisins, flaked almonds, cashews, pecans, or caramelized toffees are placed on or within sections of divided dough, which is then baked. In the United States, these are typically given a topping of fruit or sweetened cream cheese prior to baking. In Sweden, chocolate spritzing and powdered sugar are also often added above the product prior to baking. Cardamom is often added to increase the aromatic sense of sweetness.

Danish pastries as c nsumed in Denmark have different shapes and names. Some are topped with chocolate, pearl sugar, glacé icing, and/or slivered nuts and they may be stuffed with a variet of ingredients such as jam or preserves (usually apple or prune), remonce, marzipan, and/or custard. Shapes are numerous, including circles with filling in the middle (known in Denmark as Spandauers), figure –eights, spirals (known as snails), and the pretzel –like kringles.

Note: *Remonce is a creamy combination made from mixing cremed butter, flavored paste and sugar. It is used as a filling in various traditional Danish pastries and is baked along with the pastry. Remonce spread is sometimes flavored with marzipan or marzipan or almond paste.

How Danish is different from Puff pastry

There are two differences between Danish pastry and puff pastry. First of all Danish pastries contain a high level of fat of about 40%. The second difference is that Danish dough contains yeast and that isn't the case for puff pastry. This is the reason that after baking, puff pastries contain a more airy structure and a more crispy bite.

Recipe of Danish pastry:

Ingredients –

- Unsalted butter, softened –2 cups
- All –purpose flour – 1 cup
- Milk –2 cups
- White sugar – ½ cup
- Salt –2 tsp
- Active dry yeast – 4 tsp
- All –purpose flour – 8 cups
- Eggs –2 nos
- Lemon extract –1 tsp
- Almond extract –1 tsp

Method

- In a medium bowl, cream together the butter and 2/3 cup of flour. Divide into 2 equal parts, and roll each half between 2 pieces of waxed paper into a 6 x12 inch sheet. Refrigerate.
- In a large bowl, mix together the dry yeast and 3 cups of the remaining flour. In a small saucepan over medium heat, combine the milk, sugar and salt. Heat to 115 degrees F (43 degrees C), or just warm, but not hot to the touch.
- Mix the warm milk mixture into the flour and yeast along with the eggs, a extracts. Stir for 3 minutes. Knead in the remaining flour ½ dough is firm and pliable. Set aside to rest until double in size.
- Cut the dough in half, and roll each half out to a 14 inch square. Place one sheet of the cold butter onto each piece of dough, and fold the dough over it like the cover

of a book.

- Seal edges by pressing with fingers. Roll each piece out to a 20x 12 inch rectangle, and then fold into thirds by folding the long sides in over the center.
- Repeat rolling into a large rectangle and folding into thirds. Wrap in plastic and refrigerate for at least 30 minutes.
- Remove from the refrigerator one at a time, and roll and fold each piece two more times. Return to the refrigerator to chill again before shaping. If the butter gets too warm, the dough will become difficult to manage.
- To make Danishes, roll the dough out to ¼ inch thickness. The dough can be cut into squares, with a filling placed in the center.
- Fold 2 of the corners over the center to form a filled diamond shape. Or, fold the piece in half, cut into 1 inch strips, stretch, twist and roll into a spiral. Place a dollop of preserves or other filling in the center.
- Place Danishes on an ungreased baking sheet, and let rise until doubled. Preheat the oven to 450 degrees F (220 degrees C).
- Danishes can be brushed with egg white for a shiny finish.
- Bake for 8 to 10 minutes in the preheated oven, or until the bottoms are golden brown.

CHAPTER FOUR

CROISSANTS

Croissants are a style of crescent shaped Viennoiserie pastries of Austria.Viennoiseries in French comes from the word "Viennois" for people and things from Vienna. The legend takes place during the Ottoman Turk siege of the city; a baker apparently heard the Turks tunneling under the walls of the city as he lit his ovens to bake the morning bread. He quickly sounded an alarm, and the military collapsed the tunnel, saving the city. To celebrate, the baker baked crescent bread'kipferl', in the crescent moon shaped shape of the the Turkish flag.

For Austrians, eating a kipferl was a culinary re—enactment of victory over the Turks – eating their enemy. The kipferl was believed to be the spiritual ancestor of the croissant.

Austrian based, the kipferl is a crescent shaped made plain, with morning sweet nuts or other fillings. It is a denser and less flaky bread, made with a softer dough. The history of the kipferl dates back to the 13th century where it is referenced as a "sweet" and wasn't until the mid −16th century that the Austrian treat became part of the 'morning pastry' category.

The kipferl made its way to France in 1770 when Austrian –born Marie –Antoinette was offered in marriage to the future Louis XVI. Marie –Antoinette felt homesick when she arrived in France and missed Austrian cuisine. The royal bakers decided to make kipferl in her honor, which they subsequently named, "croissant." Wherever the croissant originally came from, it is firmly ensconced in French bakery tradition today.It is not to be confused with the British croissant, which is straight.

The French have remained faithful to the original Austrian crescent shape.In the first half of the 20th century, the croissant was baked and beloved by adoring French bakers and all who enjoyed it. After World War 2, the rise of mass –produced food only boosted the pastry's popularity in France, Europe and the world over.

By the end of the 20th century, the croissant took the foodservice industry by storm thanks to the introduction of flash freeze technologies, with take away 'croissanteries' and fast –food chains now able to sell croissant breakfast sandwiches and savoury pastries.Croissants fall into that category of "laminated pastry". This means the dough gets folded over and over again, with cold butter in between each tissue –thin layer. Today, the reach of the croissant goes far and wide with France, Austria, Argentina, Italy, Poland, America, Australia and many other countries having notable and delicious variants.

Recipe

Ingredients –

- Active dry yeast – 1 tsp
- Warm water ($10^0F/45^0C$)– 3 tbsps

- White sugar – 1 tsp
- All –purpose flour –1 cups
- White sugar – 1 tsp
- Salt –1 tsp
- Warm milk – 2 Cups
- Vegetable oil –2 tbsp
- Unsalted butter, chilled – 1 cup
- Egg –1no
- Water – 1 tbsp

Method –

- Combine yeast, warm water, and 1 tsp sugar. Allow to stand until creamy and frothy.
- Measure flour into a mixing bowl. Dissolve 2 tsps sugar and salt in warm milk. Blend into flour along with yeast and oil.
- Mix well; knead until smooth. Cover, and let rise until over triple in volume, about 3 hours.
- Deflate gently, and let rise again until doubled, about another 3 hours. Deflate and chill 20 minutes.
- Massage butter until pliable, but not soft and oily. Pat dough into a 14x8 –inch rectangle.
- Smear butter over top two thirds, leaving ¼ –inch margin all around.
- Fold unbuttered third over middle third, and buttered top third down over that. Turn 90 degrees, so that folds are to left and right.
- Roll out to a 14x6 –inch rectangle. Fold in three again. Sprinkle lightly with flour, and put dough in a plastic bag.

- Refrigerate 2 hours. Unwrap, sprinkle with flour, and deflate gently. Roll to a 14x6 –inch rectangle, and fold again.
- Turn 90 degrees, and repeat. Wrap, and chill 2 hours.

- To shape, roll dough out to a 20x5 –inch rectangle. Cut in half crosswise, and chill half while shaping the other half.
- Roll out to a 15 x 5 inch rectangle. Cut into three 5 x 5 inch squares.
- Cut each square in half diagonally. Roll each triangle lightly to elongate the point, and make it 7 inches long.
- Grab the other 2 points, and stretch them out slightly as you roll it up. Place on a baking sheet, curving slightly into crescent shape.
- Let shaped croissants rise until puffy and light. In a small bowl, beat together egg and 1 tbsp water.
- Glaze croissants with egg wash.
- Bake in a preheated 475^0F (245^0C) oven for 12 to 15 minutes.

CHAPTER FIVE

COFFEE CAKE DOUGH PRODUCTS

Although a few early coffee cake recipes actually called for coffee as an ingredient, the term "coffee cake" generally refers to a type of simple, usually unfrosted cake that is an accompaniment to coffee, rather than a cake that contains coffee. Coffee cake is something you would serve at breakfast or at an informal occasion such as a gathering of friends over coffee, as opposed to a fancier, gooey, layered, filled, and frosted cake that would be served as a more formal dessert.

Coffee cakes are usually made with either sweet or Danish dough and are filled with a varietyof items such as fruits, nuts, and smears. They can be made up into many sizes and shapes according to the needs of the bakeshop. There are many ways to shape coffee cakes as well:Wreathed, braided, or twisted are common methods seen with these cakes.

Wreath Coffee Cake –

- Using a sweet dough or Danish dough, make a filled dough roll, as for cinnamon rolls, but do not cut into separate pieces. Other fillings, such as prune or date, may be used instead of butter and cinnamon sugar.
- Shape the roll into a circle (a). Place on a greased baking sheet. Cut partway through the dough at 1 –in. (2.5 –cm) intervals (b). Twist each segment outward to open the cuts (c).
- Egg –wash after proofing. Bake at 375°F (190°C).

Filled Coffee Cake –

- Scale sweet dough or Danish dough into 12 –oz (340 –g) units.
- Roll each unit into a rectangle 9 × 18 in. (23 × 46 cm).
- Spread half of each rectangle with about 170 gm desired filling.
- Fold the unspread half over the spread half to make a 9 –in. (23 –cm) square.
- Place in a greased 9 –in. (23 –cm) square pan.
- Sprinkle with streusel topping, about 110 gm per pan.
- Proof
- Bake at 375°F (190°C).
-

Loaf Coffee Cake –

- Using rich sweet doughdough, make a filled dough roll, as for cinnamon rolls, using desired filling.

- Fold the roll in half, and then twist it up.
- Place the twisted roll in a greased loaf pan, or coil the twist like a snail and place in a round pan.
- Proof, wash with melted butter, and bake at 350°F (175°C).
-

Danish Pretzel –

- Using almond filling, make up Danish dough into a long, thin dough roll, as for cinnamon rolls.
- Twist the roll into a pretzel shape. Place on a sheet pan.
- Proof, egg –wash, and bake at 375°F (190°C).

Strip Coffee Cake or Danish Strip –

- Roll out the Danish dough about ¼ in. (6 mm) thick into a rectangle the length of the desired strip and about twice as wide.
- Spread the desired filling length wise down the center of the dough, leaving a ½–in. (1–cm) margin at both ends.
- Brush both ends and one edge of the rectangle with egg wash, to seal the seams.
- Fold the side of the rectangle without the egg wash over the center of the filling. Fold the other side over the center, overlapping the first side by ½ in. (1 cm).
- Turn the strip over and place it seam side down on a paper –lined pan. Make 5 or 6 diagonal slashes in the top of the dough; cut through to the filling but not to the

bottom layer of dough.
- Proof, egg –wash, and bake at 375°F (190°C).

Danish Spiral Coffee Cake –

- Using desired filling, make up Danish dough into a filled dough roll, as for cinnamon rolls, but longer and thinner.
- Flatten the roll slightly with a rolling pin. Make 2 parallel cuts lengthwise through the dough; cut through the bottom layer leaving about 1 in. (2.5 cm) uncut at both ends.
- Twist the strip as for Danish Twists. Coil the twist into a spiral. Tuck the loose end underneath to secure it.
- Proof and egg –wash. If desired, sprinkle with chopped or sliced nuts.
- Bake at 375°F (190°C).

CHAPTER SIX

YEAST RAISED SPECIALTY CAKES

What is cake ? Cake may be explained in one line as "an item of soft sweet food made from a mixture of flour, fat, eggs, sugar, and other ingredients, baked and sometimes iced or decorated."

A sweet baked good with flour, fat, eggs and sugar. But does that mean it can be raised with both baking powder/soda as well as yeast? Here is where disagreements online start popping up.

When does a cake become bread? This is where things start becoming very tricky. As you will see further on, yeast –leavened cakes tend to be less crumbly and have a firmer structure than a basic pound cake which is light and crumbly. When have you changed the structure such that it has turned into bread?

Some that bakes are called breads, but some say a brioche is a bread, others would say this is a cake. Some say a babka is a bread, others say it is a cake.

So exactly what is a cake? A cake to us has to be sweeter than bread and has to contain some sort of flour (doesn't have to be wheat). You can eat a cake without anything else, it doesn't need a topping, but it can be decorated with an icing for instance. A cake is more of a snack, whereas bread is more part of a meal. You can eat one or two slices of cake, but you can easily eat several slices of bread. Also, a cake is made from a batter, whereas bread is made from dough and requires extensive kneading. We can also think about croissant and doughnuts – croissants are pastry, probably because they use layering to incorporate air, but what about doughnuts. So the definition of cake is not so perfect, but we can go on.

Specialty Rolls: Specialty rolls include bread rolls and cake rolls. A bread roll is a small, usually round or oblong individual loaf of bread served as a meal accompaniment (eaten plain or with butter) found in most cuisines all over the world. A roll can be served and eaten whole or cut transversely and dressed with filling between the two halves. Rolls are also commonly used to make sandwiches similar to those produced using slices of bread. It's believed that the first roll was created in the south east of England in 1581. Bakers in different towns and cities used to name their bread rolls according to how they made the dough, the size of the rolls and how they baked them.

Some of the common bread rolls are as:

- *Bun* – A bun is a small, sometimes sweet, bread –based roll. Though they come in many shapes and sizes, they are most commonly hand –sized or smaller, with a round top and flat bottom.Buns are usually made from flour, sugar, milk, yeast and butter. Common sweet varieties contain small fruit or nuts, and may topped with icing or caramel, or filled with jam or cream. Some types of buns are filled with various meats, or used to serve meats (such as hotdogs or hamburgers).

- *Sweet roll* – A sweet roll or sweet bun refers to any of a number of sweet, baked, yeast –leavened breakfast or dessert foods. They may contain spices, nuts, candied fruits, etc., and are often glazed or topped with icing. Compared to regular bread dough, sweet roll dough generally has higher levels of sugar, fat, eggs, and yeast. They are often round, and are small enough to comprise a single serving.

- *Breakfast roll* – The breakfast roll is a bread roll filled with elements of a traditional fried breakfast. It typically consists of a bread roll or baguette containing one or more fillings such as sausages, bacon, white or black pudding, butter, mushrooms, tomatoes and tomato sauce or brown sauce. In some cases a hash brown, baked beans or fried egg may be added.

- *Concha* – are known for their shell –like shape and sugar shell pattern on the top. It is similar to Japanese melon pan. This is one of the most famous Mexican pastries and widely recognized in the United States. It is also referred to as "*pan de huevo*" (egg bread) in other Latin American countries, such as Chile, where they are eaten during tea time or at the beach.They are known as *Cemitas* in Honduras.

- *Hamburger bun* – is a sandwich consisting of one or more cooked patties of ground meat, usually beef, placed inside a sliced bread roll or bun. The patty may be pan fried, grilled, smoked or flame broiled. Hamburgers are often served with cheese, lettuce, tomato, onion, pickles, bacon, or chiles; condiments such as ketchup, mustard, mayonnaise, relish, or a *"special sauce"*, often a variation of

Thousand Island dressing; and are frequently placed on sesame seed buns. A hamburger topped with cheese is called a cheeseburger.

- *Hot dog bun* – is a type of soft elongated round bun shaped specifically to contain a hot dog or another type of sausage. The bun allows eaters consume hot dogs without burning their hands.
- *Challah Roll* – is a special bread in Jewish cuisine, usually braided and typically eaten on ceremonial occasions such as Shabbat and major Jewish holidays (other than Passover). Ritually –acceptable challah is made of dough from which a small portion has been set aside as an offering.
- *Parker House roll* – s a bread roll made by flattening the center of a ball of dough with a rolling pin so that it becomes an oval shape and then folding the oval in half. They are made with milk and are generally quite buttery, soft, and slightly sweet with a crispy shell. They were invented at the Parker House Hotel in Boston, during the 1870s.
- *Fruit bun* – Fruit buns are a type of sweet roll made with fruit, fruit peel, spices and sometimes nuts. They are a tradition in Britain and former British colonies

including Jamaica, Australia, Singapore and India. They are made with fruit and fruit peel and are similar to bath buns, which are sprinkled and cooked with sugar nibs. One variety is a currant bun.

- *French roll* – a circular or oval bread roll having a hard or crispy crust. Also called French twist. Named after a coiffure for women in which the hair is combed back from the face and arranged in a vertical roll on the back of the head.
- **Roll cake**: A roll cake is a cake that is rolled. A roll cake is often called a Swiss roll, jelly roll, roll cake, cream roll, or Swiss log. It's a type of sponge cake that is filled with whipped cream, jam or frosting and then rolled into a spiral before serving. A roll cake is similar to a roulade but a roulade can be filled with other things besides sweet fillings and can even be savory. The origins of the term are unclear. In spite of the name "Swiss roll", the cake is believed to have originated in the nineteenth century elsewhere in Europe, likely Austria.

Swiss roll variations:

- Swiss roll – This Swedish rolled cake has layere of delicacy egg in combination with chocolate of sweetened butter flavoring. It also has a whipped cream filling.
- In India it is called jam rolls as the inner filling is of varied jams.
- In Indonesia, the Swiss roll cake is called *bolu gulung*. Most bakeries sell Swiss rolls daily, and they are filled with butter cream, cheese or fruit jam.

- In Japan, Swiss rolls are called "roll cake". They are filled with whipped cream and sometimes with fruits like strawberries.
- In Colombia, a Swiss roll is called either *pionono* or *brazo de reina* ("queen's arm"), and it is filled with guava jam.
- In Portugal, desserts called tortas are simply Swiss rolls with jam filling.
- In Spain, the dessert is called *brazo de gitano* and is commonly filled with cream or chocolate truffle.
- In United Kingdom *Jam roly –poly* is a similar dessert, but made as pudding rather than a cake, filled with jam and served hot with custard.

Yeast raised cakes: These types of cakes are not generally referred to as yeast –leavened specifically; instead, they tend to be long –standing traditional recipes (e.g. *Kugelhopf*) from specific countries with their own names. They just happen to use yeast.

Characteristic for yeast raised cakes: As the yeast in the batter reproduces and produces carbon dioxide gas creates the little air bubbles in the cake (fermentation). In doughs this process takes place easily and quickly, but in case of cakes, it tends to contain quite a lot of butter and eggs. This slows down the growth of the yeast even more. In general, baking powder or baking soda is mostly used as they tend to make the cake light and slightly crumbly in texture. Here the aeration occurs at the same time that the proteins denature and the starches cook, which helps the cake hold on to the air. It so happens that gluten is very good at holding onto those air bubbles. But a gluten network also makes the cake less crumbly and more bread like. So gluten and gluten development becomes an important part while baking a cake or bread. However, when you use yeast, it will be slightly less crumbly. This is because the batter is thin and incorporated with lots of butter and egg, resulting in less and tender gluten development, which has less capacity to hold on air.

Since the batter cannot hold on the hot air in between the molecules of the flour batter, so development of natural flavour and moistness is rarely seen. All the flavour come from the flavouring ingredients that are added.

Types

Gugelhopf / Guglhopf / Kugelhopf / Baba

This originally yeast leavened cake various stories about its name an come from Austria, others say from France. It is also called Baba ur Rhum or Rhum Baba in German Some stories mention royal families who liked the cake and moved it to origin. It could have other neighboring countries.

Although with varied origin, its shape remained same, shaped in circle with a hole in middle (like a Bundt pan, but with a slightly different design). No adays modern bakers simply use baking powder or soda to prepare this variety. A Rum baba or Baba au rhum is a small yeast cake saturated in syrup made with hard liquor, usually rum, and sometimes filled with whipped cream or pastry cream. It is most typically made in individual servings (about a 5 cm tall, slightly tapered cylinder) but sometimes can be made in larger forms similar to those used for Bundt cakes.

Panettone: Has its origin in Italy. It is a dome shaped sweet cake with lots of fruit fillings inside.

Bara brith: This is typical Welsh cake containing fruits. It is traditionally flavoured with tea, dried fruits and mixed spices, and is served sliced and buttered at tea time.

Savarin: A savarin ith its origin in France is somewhat similar to brioche but ring like shape, but makes a lot drier bake which is why it needs to be soaked in syrup.

Recipe of Baba au Rhum Ingredients –

For the Cake:

- Dry yeast– 1 tbsp
- Water (warm) – 3 tbsp
- Eggs (beaten) – 3 nos
- All –purpose flour– 2 cups
- Granulated sugar– 2 tbsp
- Orange zest– 1 tsp
- Lemon zest– 1 tsp
- Salt– 1 tsp
- Butter (softened) – ½ cup
- Golden raisins (or dried currants) – 3/4 cup
- Dark rum– 3 tbsp
-

For the Rum Syrup:

- Water– 3 cups
- Granulated sugar– 2 cups
- Dark rum (to taste) – ½ to 2/3 cup
- Vanilla extract– 1 ½ tsp
- Apricot preserves (heated) – 2/3 cup

Garnish:

- Sweetened whipped cream– as required

Method –

To make the Cake

- Gather the ingredients.
- Stir the yeast and the warm water together in a large bowl and allow the yeast to dissolve for 5 minutes.
- Lightly beat the eggs into the yeast and water.
- In a small bowl, mix the flour, sugar, citrus zests, and salt together.
- Stir the mixture into the yeast and eggs.
- Knead the dough with the softened butter for about 5 minutes, until it turns soft and elastic.
- Cover the dough and allow it to rise for 1 hour until it doubles in size.
- While the dough is rising, soak the raisins or currants in 3 tbsps of rum.
- Once the dough has doubled, beat the rum –soaked fruit into it.
- Grease the baba molds and divide the dough among them.
- Preheat an oven to 400°F.
- Cover the molds and allow the dough to rise for 30 to 45 minutes, or until the dough has just started to rise above the molds' edges.
- Uncover the babas and bake them for 20 to 25 minutes, until they turn golden brown and begin to pull away from the sides of the molds.
- Immediately remove the babas from the molds and allow them to cool on a wire rack.

To make the Rum Syrup

- Gather the ingredients.
- While the babas are cooling, make the rum soaking syrup. In a medium saucepan set over medium heat, bring the water and sugar to a boil for 5 to 10 minutes, until the syrup has thickened.
- Remove the syrup from the heat and stir the rum and vanilla extract into the mixture.

To assemble the Rum Baba

- Place the babas into the hot rum syrup and turn them several times, allowing them to soak up the syrup. They will swell and absorb most of the syrup.
- Carefully transfer each baba onto a dessert plate and brush with a generous amount of heated apricot preserves.
- Garnish the babas au rhum with vanilla Chantilly cream and serve immediately.

Recipe of Savarin

Ingredients –

For the savarin

- Plain flour–350gm
- Caster sugar–50gm
- Instant yeast–10gm
- Salt– ½ tsp

- Milk–3 tbsp
- Eggs–6 nos
- Unsalted butter –180gm
- Orange, finely grated zest and segmented fruit–1

For the syrup

- Caster sugar –300g
- Lemon juice – 1 tbsp
- Orange liqueur –100 ml

For the chocolate disc

- Plain chocolate, finely chopped –100gm
- White chocolate, melted –50gm
-

For the caramel chards

- Caster sugar –150gm

For the Chantilly cream

- Double cream – 300ml
- Icing sugar 15gm
- Vanilla essence – ½ tsp

To decorate

- Sliced mixed fruit (such as orange, mango, kiwi, strawberries) pomegranate seeds, blueberries or raspberries.

Method –

- Stir together the flour, sugar and yeast in a large bowl. Mix the salt, milk and eggs together in a jug then pour into the flour mixture and beat well using a wooden spoon for about 5 minutes to make a thick, sticky batter.
- Gradually add the butter, beating until the mixture is smooth, elastic and shiny. Finally fold in the orange and lemon zest. Cover the bowl with cling film and leave to rise for 1 hour.
- For the syrup, tip the sugar into a pan, add the lemon juice and 150ml/5fl oz water and bring to a simmer, stirring until the sugar dissolves. Remove from the heat, stir in the orange liqueur and leave to cool.
- For the chocolate disc, temper the plain chocolate by melting three –quarters (75g/2 ½oz) of the chocolate over a pan of simmering water (do not let the bottom of the bowl touch the water). Stir until the chocolate reaches a melting temperature of 50C. Remove the bowl from the heat, add the remaining chocolate and stir until it's cooled to 31C.
- Spoon into a piping bag made out of baking parchment and pipe a 5cm/2in oval disc onto a sheet of baking paper or acetate and leave to set. Spoon the melted white chocolate into another piping bag and pipe the word 'Savarin' onto the plain chocolate disc.
- For the caramel shards, line a baking tray with silicone or baking parchment. Add the sugar to a pan with 4 tbsps water and bring to a simmer, stirring until the sugar dissolves. When all the sugar is dissolved, bring the syrup to a boil without stirring until it reaches 170C

on a sugar thermometer (CAUTION: boiling sugar is extremely hot. Handle very carefully). Immediately pour out onto the lined tray and leave to harden. Crack with a spoon or cut into shards using a knife.

- Grease a 23 cm/ 9 innches bundt tin or savarin mould with butter. When the batter has risen, spoon it into the tin. Cover with oiled clingfilm and leave to rise for 45 minutes to 1 hour, until it reaches three –quarters of the way up the tin.
- Preheat the oven to 180⁰C / 160⁰C.
- Remove the cling film and bake for 20–25 minutes or until the savarin is risen and golden –brown. Remove from the oven and place the tin on a wire rack to cool for 5–10 minutes.
- When cool enough to handle, remove the savarin from the tin and pour half of the syrup into the tin. Gently place the savarin back into the tin to soak up the syrup and cool completely. Pour the remaining syrup into a roasting tin, then place the savarin into the syrup and leave to soak for 5 minutes. Carefully transfer to a serving plate.
- Meanwhile, for the Chantilly cream, whip the cream, icing sugar and vanilla together until soft peaks form when the whisk is removed. Spoon one –third of the Chantilly cream into a piping bag fitted with a star nozzle. Set aside in the fridge until ready to serve.
- Using a sharp knife, segment the zested orange. Carefully slice off the top and bottom of the orange. Using even downward strokes, slice the skin away from the flesh and discard. Remove any remaining white pith.
- Pipe the Chantilly cream around the top of the savarin and arrange the orange slices over the cream. Fill the savarin with the remaining Chantilly cream and

decorate with sliced fruit. Top with the chocolate disc and caramel shards.

• 31 •

CHAPTER SEVEN

BUNS

A bun is a small, sometimes sweet, bread –based item or roll. Though they come in many shapes and sizes, they are most commonly hand –sized or smaller, with a round top and flat bottom. Buns are usually made from flour, sugar, milk, yeast, butterand occasionally egg. Common sweet varieties contain small fruit or nuts, and may topped with icing or caramel, or filled with jam or cream. Some types of buns are filled with various meats, or used to serve meats (such as hotdogs or hamburgers). "Bun" may also refer to particular types of filled dumplings, such as Chinese *baozi*. Some of these types of dumplings may be bread –like in texture. They are also called Dinner roll in England.

Difference between bread and a bun:

Without any of the one item mentioned, the dough remains to be 'bread dough' rather than 'bun dough'.Bread is usually baked in a loaf which serves serveral people (or several servings for one person). A bun is a single –serving baked good. The recipes may be identical, but the shape and size determine the difference. The weight of both of the two also matters. As per the bread laws existed in all bread eating cultures and they have defined the permissible weights of loaves of bread. Typically there has been a minimum weight for the smallest legal loaf and anything below that weight is a *bun* (in English), a *petit pain* (in French) or a *Broetchen* (in German). Traditionally the line has been either one or two pounds, which was then later redefined in grams. In the UK Bread Act of 1822 a loaf of bread was required to be 2 or 4 lbs, for example. In France and Germany a bun is still defined as a small bread of up to 250 grams.

Some of the common buns include:

1. **Anpan** – A bun that is filled, usually with red bean paste, or with white beans, sesame, or chestnut
2. **Bakpao** – Indonesian term for steamed bun. The bun is usually filled with pork, but can also be filled with other ingredients, such as chicken, peanuts, or mung beans.
3. **Bánh bao** – Vietnamese meaning "Enveloping Cake", which is a ball –shaped bun containing pork or chicken meat, onions, eggs, mushrooms and vegetables, in the Vietnamese cuisine
4. **Baozi** – A type of steamed, filled bun or bread –like item made with baker's yeast in various Chinese cuisines, as there is much variation as to the fillings and the preparations
5. **Blaa** – A dough –like, white bread bun (roll) speciality particularly associated with Waterford, Ireland; historically, the blaa is also believed to have been made in Kilkenny and Wexford.
6. **Bread roll** – A short, oblong, or round bun served usually before or with meals, often with butter.

7. **Bunuelo** — A fried dough ball popular in Latin America, Greece, Guam, Turkey, Israel and Morocco. It will usually have a filling or a topping.

8. **Cheese bun** – A variety of small, baked, cheese –flavored rolls, a popular snack and breakfast food in Bolivia, Brazil (especially in the state of Minas Gerais), Paraguay, Colombia and northern Argentina.

9. **Chelsea bun** – A currant bun that is first created in the 18th century at the Chelsea Bun House in Chelsea, London, an establishment favoured by Hanoverian royalty which was demolished in 1839.

10. **Cinnamon bun** – A sweet roll served commonly in Northern Europe and North America; its main ingredients are dough, cinnamon, sugar, and butter, which provide a robust and sweet flavor

11. **Cocktail bun** – A Hong Kong –style sweet bun with a filling of shredded coconut; one of several iconic types of baked goods originating from Hong Kong.

12. **Cream bun** – A bun that varies all around the world; typically they are made with an enriched dough bread roll that is baked and cooled, then split and filled with cream.

13. **Curry bread** – Some Japanese curry is wrapped in a piece of dough, which is coated in flaky bread crumbs, and usually deep fried or baked.

14. **Dampfnudel** – A white bread roll or sweet roll eaten as a meal or as a dessert in Germany and in France (Alsace); a typical dish in southern Germany.

15. **Fruit bun** – A sweet roll made with fruit, fruit peel, spices and sometimes nuts; a tradition in Britain and former British colonies including Jamaica, Australia, Singapore, and India.

16. **Hamburger bun** – A round bun designed to encase a hamburger; invented in 1916 by a fry cook named Walter Anderson, who co –founded White Castle in 1992.

17. **Hot cross bun** – A sweet, spiced bun usually made with fruit but with other varieties such as apple –cinnamon or maple syrup and blueberries and marked with a cross on the top, traditionally eaten on Good Friday in the UK, Australia, New Zealand, South Africa, and Canada, but now popular all year round.

18. **Hot dog bun** – A long, soft bun shaped specifically to contain a hot dog or frankfurter.

19. **Mandarin roll** – A steamed bun originating from China; cooked by steaming; a food staple of Chinese cuisine which is similar to white bread in western cuisine.

20. **Piggy bun** – A Hong Kong pastry that is essentially the equivalent of the French baguette; found in Hong Kong bakeries and Cha chaan teng; in Hong Kong, it is often cut in half and served with butter and condensed milk.

21. **Pork chop bun** – famous and popular snack in Macau, the "piggy bun" is crisp outside and soft inside; a freshly fried pork chop is filled into it

22. **Rum roll** – historic Washington D.C. specialty, similar to a cinnamon bun with rum flavored icing.

23. **Sally Lunn bun** – A enriched yeast bread associated with the city of Bath in the West Country of England.

24. **Semla** – A traditional sweet roll made in various forms in Denmark, the Faroe Islands, Iceland, Estonia, Finland, Latvia, Lithuania, Sweden and Norway; associated with Lent and especially Shrove Monday and Shrove Tuesday; the oldest version of the semla was a plain bread bun, eaten in a bowl of warm milk; in Swedish this is known as *Hetvägg*

25. **Shengjian mantou** – A type of small, pan –fried baozi which is a specialty of Shanghai and usually filled with pork and gelatin that melts into soup/liquid when cooked.
26. **Siopao** – Hokkien term for baozi, literally meaning "steamed buns"; it has also been incorporated into Thai cuisine where it is called salapao.
27. **Sufganiyah** – A deep –fried bun, filled with jam or custard, and then topped with powdered sugar. Typically eaten in Israel during Hanukkah.
28. **Sticky bun** – A dessert or breakfast sweet roll that generally consists of rolled pieces of leavened dough, sometimes containing brown sugar or cinnamon, which are then compressed together to form a flat loaf corresponding to the size of the baking pan; they have been consumed since the Middle Ages, at which time cinnamon became more prominent.
29. **Teacake** – A fruited sweet bun usually served toasted and buttered.
30. **Tingmo** – Steamed bread in Tibetan cuisine. It is sometimes described as a steamed bun that is similar to Chinese flower rolls. It does not contain any kind of filling.
31. **Xiaolongbao** – A steamed bun from the Jiangnan region of China; fillings vary by region and usually include some meat and/or a gelatin –gelled aspic that becomes a soup when steamed.
32. **Zeeuwse bolus** – A spiral shaped bun covered in dark brown sugar, lemon zest and cinnamon.

Recipe
Ingredients –

- Active dry yeast –25 gm
- All –purpose flour –1 kg
- Lukewarm water –1 cup
- Large egg –1no
- Melted butter –3 tbsp
- White sugar –3 tbsp
- Salt –1¼ tsps
- Refined oil –1 tsp
- Beaten egg –1 no
- Milk –1 tbsp
- Sesame seeds –1 tsp

Method –

- Line a baking sheet with a silicone mat or parchment paper.
- Place yeast into bowl of a large stand mixer; whisk in ½cup flour and warm water until smooth. Let stand until mixture is foamy, 10 to 15 minutes.
- Whisk 1 egg, melted butter, sugar, and salt thoroughly into yeast mixture. Add remaining flour (about 3 cups).
- Fit a dough hook onto stand mixer and knead the dough on low speed until soft and sticky, 5 to 6 minutes. Scrape sides if needed. Poke and prod the dough with a silicone spatula; if large amounts of dough stick to the spatula, add a little more flour.
- Transfer dough onto a floured work surface; dough will be sticky and elastic but not stick to your fingers. Form the dough lightly into a smooth, round shape, gently tucking loose ends underneath.
- Wipe out stand mixer bowl, drizzle olive oil into the bowl, and turn dough over in the bowl several times to coat surface thinly with oil. Cover bowl with aluminum

foil. Let dough rise in a warm place until doubled, about 2 hours.

- Transfer dough to a floured work surface and pat to flatten bubbles and form into a slightly rounded rectangle of dough about 5x10 inches and about ½ inch thick. Dust dough lightly with flour if needed. Cut dough into 8 equal pieces. Form each piece into a round shape, gently tucking ends underneath as before.
- Use your hands to gently pat and stretch the dough rounds into flat disc shapes about ½ inch thick. Arrange buns about ½ inch apart on prepared baking sheet. Dust buns very lightly with flour. Drape a piece of plastic wrap over the baking sheet (do not seal tightly). Let buns rise until doubled, about 1 hour.
- Preheat oven to 375 degrees F (190 degrees C).
- Beat 1 egg with milk in a small bowl, using a fork, until mixture is thoroughly combined. Very gently and lightly brush tops of buns with egg wash without deflating the risen dough. Sprinkle each bun with sesame seeds.
- Bake in the preheated oven until lightly browned on top, 15 to 17 minutes. Buns will stick together slightly where they touch. Let cool completely, tear the buns apart, and slice in half crosswise to serve.

CHAPTER EIGHT

DOUGHNUTS AND CRULLERS

Doughnuts are deep –fried round wheel or ring shaped cakes or confectionary with a hole and with roots in European history in the Middle Eastern cuisine. They were introduced to America by the Dutch as *oliekoecken* (oil cakes or fried cakes). Another history illustrates that in ancient Rome and Greece, cooks would fry strips of pastry dough and coat them with honey or fish sauce.

In Medieval times, Arab cooks started frying up small portions of unsweetened yeast dough, drenching the plain fried blobs in sugary syrup to sweeten them. These Arab fritters spread into northern Europe in the 1400's and became very popular Europe. Doughnuts are made of yeast dough rich in eggs and butter, spices and dried fruits, their sweetness came from the fruit and the final dusting of sugar.

The original spelling for this fried good that first appeared in print back in the early 19th Century was '*doughnut.*' This combination of the words dough and nut was used because doughnuts were initially nut –sized balls of sweet dough deep –fried in oil or fat. The word 'nut' was used in the earlier context of referring to small rounded cake or cookies.

It is called 'doughnut' in internationally, but 'donut' only in America.The holes became a necessity and were added to the center of the fritter. This was because the fritters would often end up raw in the center after frying– the exterior would cook before the inner part of the doughnut did. The addition of a hole in the center eliminated that problem. In some parts of America and Middle Europe doughnuts are also made in the shape of balls, fingers and stars.

Once fried, doughnuts may be glazed with a sugar icing, spread with icing or chocolate on top, or topped with powdered sugar, cinnamon, sprinkles or fruit and are filled with custards or fruit preserves. Other shapes include rings, balls, flattened spheres, twists, and other forms.

Leavening agents in doughnuts –

Doughnuts are prepared by using two types of leavening agents – natural leavening agents like yeast and chemical leavening agent like baking soda.

- Yeast –raised donuts that use yeast and fermentation to obtain its volume.
- Cake donuts that are chemically leavened (usually with a leavening agent and sodium bicarbonate)

Yeast raised Doughnuts: Yeast or raised (because the dough is raised) donuts, are your classic glazed donut. The dough is mixed with live yeast inside of it and it is cut out into a shape before being fried to golden colour. They're light and airy, but have a chew and a slight yeast flavor. The unique characteristics of donuts are their traditional ring shape and the method of frying in hot oil. Yeast –leavened donuts are porous, resilient and have a bread –like crumb structure. There are few variation according to their shaps ans sizes, like:

- *Rings:* conventional donut with a hole in the middle
- *Twists:* made by braiding or twisting one or two pieces of dough together
- *Honey buns:* cinnamon swirled rolls
- *Shells:* round and usually filled with jelly or cream
- *Long johns:* rectangular shape

The mixing method used to prepare yeast –raised doughnuts is the modified straight dough method.

The dough used for yeast doughnuts is similar to regular sweet dough or bun dough, except it is often not as rich—that is, doughnuts are made with less fat, sugar, and eggs. Doughs that are too rich will brown too fast and absorb too much frying fat. The finished products will be greasy and either too dark on the outside or insufficiently cooked inside. Also, a leaner dough has stronger gluten, which can better withstand the handling involved in proofing and frying.

After fermentation, bring the dough to the bench in sufficient time to allow for makeup. Remember that fermentation continues during makeup. If the dough gets too old (proofed too long), the doughnuts will require longer frying to become browned and thus will be greasier. When you are preparing a large quantity of doughnuts, it may be necessary to place some of the dough in the retarder so it doesn't become old.

Watch the dough temperature carefully, especially in warm weather if the dough is much above 80°F (24°C), it will become old more quickly.

Proof the doughnuts at a lower temperature and humidity than you do breads. Some bakers proof them at room temperature, if there is a part of the bakeshop that isn't too hot (about 70°F/21°C). Doughnuts proofed this way are less likely to be deformed or dented when handled or brought to the fryer.

Handle fully proofed units carefully, as they are soft and easily dented. Many bakers give doughnuts only three –quarters proof. This makes a denser doughnut, but one that is easier to handle.

Heat the frying fat to the proper temperature. Fat temperature for raised doughnuts varies from 360° to 385°F (182° to 195°C), depending on the formula. Richer formulas require a lower temperature to avoid excessive browning. The formula in this book requires a frying temperature of 360° (182°C).

Arrange the proofed units on screens on which they can be lowered into fat. (For small quantities, you can place them by hand in the fryer, but take care not to burn yourself.) Frying time is about 2 ½ minutes. The doughnuts must be turned over when they are half done in order to brown evenly on both sides.

Lift from the frying fat with the screen, or, if you are frying in smaller quantities, with the frying basket or a spider, holding the doughnuts over the frying fat for a moment to let the fat drain from the doughnuts back into the kettle. Set the doughnuts on brown paper to absorb excess fat.

Recipe of yeast doughnut

Ingredients –

- Warm milk – ½ cup
- Sugar –1 tsp
- Dry yeast –1 tsp
- All purpose flour –2 cups
- Baking powder –¼ tsp
- Butter, room temperature –2 tbsp
- Salt –pinch
- Water – ½ cup water
- Refined oil to –grease & deep fry

For chocolate glaze:

- Powdered sugar –1 cup
- Cocoa powder –¼ cup
- Vanilla extract / essence –1 tsp
- Milk –3 tbsp

Method –

- Firstly, activate yeast by adding milk and sugar.
- Now add maida, baking powder, butter and salt.
- Combine and knead to smooth dough adding water as required.
- Grease, cover and rest for 1 –2 hours.
- Punch the dough and roll slightly thick using rolling pin.
- Now with the help of donut cutter, cut round.
- Allow to rest in warm place for 2 hours.
- Deep fry in medium hot oil to golden brown.

- Dip the doughnuts and serve chocolate donuts sprinkled with sugar crystals.

Cake Doughnuts: A cake donut is made with a sweetened batter that's leavened with the help of baking powder or baking soda, and is extruded into oil to cook. Cake doghnuts include apple cider donuts, chocolate cake donuts with glaze, and those crunch old fashioned donuts that are sometimes glazed and sometimes not. Cake doughnut production proceeds at very fast rates leaving a very small window between mixing and frying stages, so proper scheduling of the operations is a must. The batter dropped into the frying fat must rise to the surface (become less dense) very quickly so that it can be conveyed at the surface by the flights of the continuous fryer, or the next batter piece will be dropped on top of the previous deposited doughnut.

Automated and pre −mix batter: Operations that produce cake doughnuts in volume use equipment that drops batter directly into the hot fat. This equipment is usually automatic, although small hand −operated depositors are also available. Automatic depositors use relatively slack dough that is generally made from prepared mixes. To use these mixes and depositors, follow two important guidelines:

- Follow manufacturers' directions closely when preparing the mix.
- Keep the depositor head 1 ½ inch (4 cm) above the fat. If the doughnut must drop much farther than this into the fat, poor shape may result.
- Operations that make cake doughnuts by hand use a stiffer mix that is rolled out and cut with cutters.

Follow these guidelines when preparing cake doughnuts:

1. Scale ingredients carefully. Even small errors can result in products with unsatisfactory texture or appearance.
2. Mix the dough until smooth, but do not overmix. Undermixed doughs result in a rough appearance and excessive fat absorption. Overmixed doughs result in tough, dense doughnuts.
3. Dough temperature should be about 70° to 75°F (21° to 24°C) when the units are fried. Be especially careful of dough temperature during hot weather.
4. Let the cutout units rest about 15 minutes before frying in order to relax the gluten.
5. Failure to relax the dough results in toughness and poor expansion.
6. Fry at the proper temperature. Normal fat temperature for cake doughnuts is 375° to 385°F (190° to 195°C). Frying time is about 1 ½ to 2 minutes. Doughnuts must be turned over when half done.

Recipe of cake doughnut

Doughnut batter: Traditionally deep –fried, cake doughnuts start with a flour batter made with baking powder, sugar, milk and butter. The batter is usually piped directly into hot oil in a doughnut shape or into doughnut molds for baking.

Ingredients –

- All –purpose flour – 2 cups

- Baking powder – 1 tsp
- Salt – ½ tsp
- Freshly grated nutmeg (optional) – ½ tsp
- Egg – 1 room temperature
- Granulated sugar –2/3 cup
- Vanilla extract –1 ½ tsp
- Unsalted butter – ½ tbsp, melted and cooled
- Buttermilk – ½ cup (or milk), at room temperature
- Vegetable, canola, or peanut oil – for frying

For the chocolate glaze:

- Unsalted butter – 100 gm
- Whole milk – ¼ cup
- Light corn syrup – 2 tsp
- Vanilla extract – 1 tbsp
- Semi –sweet chocolate – 100 gm chopped
- Powdered sugar – 2 cups sifted

Method –

- In a large bowl, mix together all the flour, baking powder, salt, and nutmeg.
- In another large bowl, use an electric mixer fitted with the paddle attachment to beat the eggs and sugar until thick and pale, about 5 minutes. Beat in the vanilla extract.
- On low speed, alternately add the flour mixture with the milk and melted butter, starting and ending with the

flour. The dough will be soft.

- Cover with plastic wrap and let sit at room temperature for 30 minutes, or until the dough is firm enough to handle.
- Turn the dough out onto a floured work surface. Roll the dough out into ¼ inch thickness and cut with a doughnut cutter or with a large round cutter and a small cutter for the holes. Place the doughnuts on a lightly floured parchment lined baking sheet. Let the doughnuts sit at room temperature while you heat the oil.
- Heat the oil in a large, deep, and heavy pan to 176°C. Place three to four doughnuts in the oil at a time and fry until golden brown, about 1 minute or less per side (30 seconds for the holes).
- Do not overcook the doughnuts. Drain on a paper towel –lined plate.

For the glaze:

- In a medium saucepan over medium heat, combine the butter, milk, corn syrup, and vanilla and heat until the butter melts. Decrease the heat to low and add the chocolate, whisking until melted. Turn off the heat and add the powdered sugar, whisking until smooth.
- Immediately dip the doughnuts into the glaze. If the glaze begins to set return the saucepan to low heat and stir until liquid again. Let the glaze set on the doughnuts for 30 minutes before serving.

Preparation and Care during frying doughnuts: Properly fried doughnuts absorb about 2 ounces (60 g) of fat per dozen. Therefore, frying fat should be of good quality and properly maintained; otherwise, the quality of the doughnuts will suffer. Observe the following guidelines for care of frying fat:

1. Use good –quality, flavorless fat. The best fat for frying has a high smoke point (the temperature at which the fat begins to smoke and to break down rapidly).
2. Solid shortenings are popular for frying because they are stable and because they congeal when the doughnuts cool, making them appear less greasy. However, such doughnuts can have an unpleasant eating quality because the fat does not melt in the mouth.
3. Fry at the proper temperature. Using too low a temperature extends frying time, causing excessive greasiness.
4. If you do not have automatic equipment with thermostatic temperature controls, keep a fat thermometer clipped to the side of the frying kettle.
5. Maintain the fat at the proper level in the fryer. When additional fat must be added, allow time for it to heat.
6. Do not fry too many doughnuts at a time. Overloading will lower the fat temperature, will not allow room for expansion of the doughnuts, and will make it difficult to turn them over.
7. Keep the fat clean. Skim out food particles as necessary. After each day's use, cool the fat until it is warm, strain it, and clean the equipment.
8. Discard spent fat. Old fat loses frying ability, browns excessively, and imparts a bad flavor.
9. Keep the fat covered when not in use. Try to aerate it as little as possible when filtering.

Finishing Doughnuts: Doughnuts should be well drained and cooled before finishing with sugar or other coatings. If they are hot, steam from the doughnuts will soak the coating. The following are some popular coatings and finishes for doughnuts:

- Roll in a mixture of cinnamon and powdered sugar or simple powdered sugar.
- Ice the tops of the doughnuts with a fondant or fudge icing.
- To glaze, dip in warm Doughnut Glaze (recipe follows) or in a warmed, thinned simple icing or fondant. Place on screens until glaze sets.
- After glazing, and while glaze is still moist, doughnuts may be rolled in coconut or chopped nuts.

Some finishing options:

- **Powdered:** Toss in powdered sugar or cinnamon sugar.
- **Glazed:** Mix 3/4 cup powdered sugar, 3 to 4 tbsps heavy cream or milk (enough to make a runny glaze), and ½tsp vanilla (optional).
- **Chocolate –glazed**: Mix 3/4 cup powdered sugar, 2 tbsps dark cocoa powder, and 4 to 5 tbsps milk or cream.
- **Chocolate –coated**: Dip doughnuts in tempered chocolate thinned with 1 to 2 tbsps vegetable oil.
- **Fruit –glazed:** Mix 1 cup powdered sugar and ¼ cup fruit purée.
- **Violet –glazed:** Mix 1 cup powdered sugar, ¼ cup cream or milk, and 1 tsp violet extract. Garnish with candied violets.

- **Pistachio:** Glaze donuts with basic glaze, then press in chopped toasted pistachios.
- **Coconut: Glaze** with coconut glaze (1 cup powdered sugar, ¼ cup coconut milk, and ½tsp vanilla), and press in toasted coconut flakes.
- **Black and white:** Make a dark chocolate ganache with 1 cup chopped dark chocolate and ½ cup heavy cream. Make a white chocolate ganache with 1 cup chopped white chocolate with ¼ cup heavy cream. Glaze half the doughnut with the chocolate glaze and half with the white glaze.
- **Caramel –glazed:** Melt 1 cup of caramel candies with 1/3 cup heavy cream in the microwave in 10 –second blasts until fully melted. Thin the glaze with additional milk or cream as needed to get a pourable glaze.
- **Meyer lemon:** Mix 1 cup powdered sugar with the zest and juice of 1 Meyer lemon, then add enough milk to form a pourable glaze.
- **Cinnamon roll:** Roll out the dough to ¼ inch thick. Mix together 1 stick melted butter with 1 cup granulated sugar and 2 tbsps ground cinnamon. Spread the mixture evenly all over the dough, then roll tightly into a cylinder. Cut into 1 inch – thick pieces, then fry until golden brown. Glaze with basic glaze.

Comparison between the Yeast raised doughnuts and Cake doughnuts

1. Yeast doughnuts are made of dough, where as cake doughnuts are made of batter.

2. Yeast doughnuts, as the name clearly spells out, are made from dough leavened with yeast, whereas cake doughnuts are traditionally made from a kind of cake batter that uses a chemical leavener (i.e. baking po baking soda).

3. The dough of Yeast doughnuts are very less sweeter than that of cake batter.

4. Yeast doughnuts are lighter: Once cooked, a cross –section reveals a mosaic of air pockets, givin chewy texture. Cake the style a puffy, malleable quality, and a slightly doughnuts, on the other hand, have a dense, more compact crumb, and a sturdy, crisp exterior shell.

5. Yeast doughnuts typically get most of their flavor from the glaze or icings or the fillings, where as in Cake Doughnuts, the batter can come in different kinds of flavorings.

6. Yeast doughnuts are generally soft, fluffy with a smooth surface but with lots of bubbles high amount of fat and liquid, but cake doughnuts have small pores that lack honeycomb structure, less soft and fluffy.

7. Yeast doughnut has more chewey where as cake doughnut is much tenderer.

8. All Yeast doughnuts do not look alike, where as all cake doughnuts look alike.

9. Yeast doughnuts are pliable and so it is easier to fill with jam or cream, where as cake doughnut is not pliable and so jam or cream cannot be filled, instead they can be sandwiched between the two layers of the doughnut which has been sliced.

10. Yeast doughnuts take time to prepare as the yeast requires some time to ferment and raise the dough, whereas the baking powder in cake dough batter rises instantly and the product comes our easily. Moreover

raised donuts absorb less oil than the cake variety.

Crullers: These are rich, light disk or oblong shaped cakes, similar to doughnuts, but are made of rich dough twisted or curled, fried in deep fat and topped with white icing.Crullers are most commonly found in Canada, New England, the Mid –Atlantic and North Central states of the United States, but are also common in California. The German origin is probably why traditional crullers can be found more easily in the Midwest, where many German immigrants settled. The traditional French cruller is made from pate a choux and is basically hollow. The word "cruller" comes from the Dutch word "krulle" or "krullen," meaning twisted cake.

Difference between a cruller and a doughnut: Yeast Donuts are soft, tender with a slight fermented flavor and sweet to the taste. A Cruller has a soft, airy texture with a pleasant light "egg –like" flavor. The center of the Cruller is wet with a crunchy exterior. The shape of a proper Cruller should resemble a golden brown pinwheel.

Recipe Ingredients –

- Water –1 cup
- Unsalted butter –6 tbsp
- Superfine sugar –2 tsp
- Salt –¼ tsp
- All –purpose flour, sifted –1 cup
- Eggs –3 nos
- Slightly beaten egg whites –2 nos
- ½ –inch star pastry attachment
- Vegetable oil –for frying

For honey glaze:

- Honey – ¼ cup
- Light brown sugar –1 tbsp
- Butter –1 tbsp

Method –

- Bring the water, butter, sugar and salt to a brisk boil in a heavy –bottomed saucepan.
- Stir in the flour all at once and continue stirring until the flour is completely incorporated. Keep stirring over medium –high heat. The more moisture you can remove, the more eggs you can mix in later which will result in a lighter pastry.
- When you see a thin film start to coat the bottom of the pan, the batter is ready. Transfer the dough to the bowl of a stand mixer. Use the paddle attachment to stir the dough for a minute to help it cool. Turn the mixer to medium speed and add one egg. Don't add the next egg until the previous has been completely incorporated into the dough.
- Then add the egg whites a little bit at a time until the dough becomes smooth and glossy and holds a little shape (not much). Do not add too much egg white or else the crullers will become heavy.
- Transfer the dough to a large pastry bag fitted with a ½ –inch star tip.

- Fry the crullers in 2 inches (or more) of hot vegetable oil in a heavy –bottomed saucepan.
- While the oil is heating, cut a dozen 3 –x3 –inch squares of parchment. Lightly grease the squares on one side and pipe a ring of dough onto each of the squares.
- When the oil has reached temperature, carefully place a French cruller, paper –side up, into the hot oil maximum possible all together.
- After a minute or so, use tongs and a sharp knife tip to gently peel the parchment off the cruller.
- When the cruller turns golden (about 2 minutes), flip it over and let it fry for another couple of minutes before removing it to drain on a cooling rack or paper towels.

Make the glaze:

- While the cruller donuts cool, mix the confectioners' sugar, honey, and milk together until smooth.
- When the crullers are cool to the touch, dip the top of each cruller into the honey glaze and set on a cooling rack to let the drips run off. When the glaze has set, the crullers are ready to serve.

Crullers can also be baked.

- Preheat oven to 450°F.
- Pipe crullers onto a parchment –lined baking sheet at least 2 inches apart. Bake for five minutes then reduce oven to 350 degrees and bake another 15

minutes.
- Turn off heat, open the oven door a crack, and let crullers sit for 5 to 10 minutes.
- Glaze and serve.

Whole wheat doughnuts: The whole wheat grain when ground with the skin and germ yields brownish flour called 'atta'or whole wheat flour. The same when refined further or ground without the skin yields whiter flour called 'maida' or refined flour. Whole wheat flours contain lots of fibres and are very important for health as it is easier to digest. So nowadays bakers and confectioners have started preparing doughnuts using whole wheat flour in the recipe, either alone or with a mixture of refined flour. They are mixing whole wheat flour with refined flour to make the product. Although the texture of whole wheat flour doughnut is a bit coarser than the only refined flour doughnut, but one can easily prefer the earlier one than the later when it comes to health.

Recipe with mixture of whole wheat flour and refined flour Ingredients –

- Warm milk –1 cup
- Dry active yeast –2 tbsp
- All purpose flour –3/4 cup
- Egg yolks –3 nos
- Granulated sugar –2 tbsp
- Vanilla extract –1 tsp
- Salt – ½ tsp
- White whole wheat flour, divided –1 ½ – 1 3/4 cups
- Unsalted butter (softened) or shortening –¼ cup

- Canola oil –for frying
- Filling – peanut butter or lemon curd both
- Glaze or powdered sugar – as required

Method –

- Pour the warm milk into the mixing bowl of a stand mixer. Add the yeast and whisk until dissolved. Whisk in the all purpose flour until the mixture is smooth. Cover the bowl and let the mixture rest in a warm place for 30 minutes.
- Add the egg yolks, sugar, vanilla, salt, and ½ cup of the whole wheat flour. Using the beater blade, beat on low speed until combined and smooth. Add in the butter/shortening and continue to beat on low speed until fully incorporated.
- Switch to the dough hook attachment, and gradually add the remaining flour while beating on low speed. Add just enough flour for the dough to come together and pull away completely from the sides of the bowl. Transfer the dough to a greased bowl, cover with plastic wrap, and refrigerate overnight (or at least 6 hours).
- Once the dough has chilled and risen, turn it out onto a lightly floured surface. Roll it out to about ½ –inch thickness. Use round cookie cutters or biscuit cutters (about 2 ½ to 3 inches in diameter) to cut circles from the dough. Gather up the scraps, re –roll, and continue to cut out circles. Use a smaller cookie cutter to cut doughnut holes from the scraps if you like, as well. Transfer the round doughnuts to a baking sheet and let them rise for about 15 minutes.

- While the doughnuts rise, pour about two inches of oil into a large, deep pot. Heat the oil to about 360°F to fry the doughnuts.
- Meanwhile, line a baking sheet with paper towels and place a wire cooling rack on top of the baking sheet.
- Once the oil comes up to temperature, carefully fry the doughnuts a few at a time, making sure there is plenty of room in the pot. Fry for a minute or two on each side, until the doughnut is puffy and golden. Use a slotted spoon to remove the doughnuts from the oil and then transfer them to the cooling rack to cool.
- When the doughnuts are completely cool, they can be filled with your filling of choice using a pastry bag and a large round pastry tip and glazed or dipped in chocolate.

Recipe with only whole wheat flour Ingredients —

For Dough

- Whole Wheat Flour- 1¼ Cup Yogurt-¼ Cup
- Milk- ¼ cup or as required Sugar- 2 tbsp
- Butter-1tbsp
- Baking Powder-1tbsp Vanilla Essence- 1tbsp Salt- a pinch
- Baking soda- a pinch

For Glaze/Coating

- Powder Sugar- ½ Cup.
- Melted Butter- 2-3tbsp Warm Water- 2-3 tbsp

Method –

- Take wheat flour in a mixing bowl. Add 1 tbsp butter to it. Mix with finger tips.
- Add powdered sugar, baking Soda, baking powder, salt and vanilla essence to the mixture. Mix well.
- Add yogurt to the mixture. Mix to get a crumbled texture.
- Add required warm milk little by little to get smooth dough. Cover and set aside the dough for 15 minutes. Meanwhile, preheat the oven at 200 degree Celsius for 15 minutes.
- Dust the working surface with little flour and knead the dough again for 2 –3 minutes. Roll it into a thick circle.
- Use a doughnut cutter or use a round cookie cutter or a sharp corner round glass and cut into small disk. Take a small cap/lid of bottle, press on centre of disk and make small hole to get exact shape of doughnut.
- Place the doughnuts on a parchment paper lined baking tray. Bake for 10 –12 minutes or until golden brown in a preheated oven at 200 degree Celsius. I have baked the doughnuts in a microwave using convection mode. Keep an eye on the doughnuts while baking after 7 –8 minutes as temperature may vary from oven to oven.
- Take a small bowl for sugar glaze. Add powder sugar, melted butter, and warm water, mix it well and make syrup. Dip the baked doughnuts in the sugar syrup to coat them from all sides with the syrup. Allow to drain on a wired rack.
- Serve with coffee.

CHAPTER NINE

SHORT CRUST/ DOUGH PASTRIES

Short crust pastry is the simplest and most common pastry. It is made with flour, fat, butter, salt, sugar, water and sometimes egg and milk to bind the dough. This is used mainly in preparation of tarts, quiche or pie, biscuits and cookies. The flour should have low gluten content, one that is milled from soft wheat flour. The fat will reduce the extensibility of the gluten that is it makes the gluten strands shorter....hence the term *shortening* for the fat used in the bakery and the term *short crust pastry*. The usual method of making short crust pastry is by the rub –in method.

Chilled fat or butter is rubbed into the sieved flour so that it is finely dispersed and resembles a sandy or bread crumb like texture. The fat forms a thin layer or coating on the glutenin and gliadin molecules and results in a short (as in crumbly; hence the term shortcrust), tender pastry, without turning the fat into a continuous paste. Cold water is sprinkled over the mixture to form smooth dough.

The ratio of fat to flour is normally 1:2, but the fat can be increased to equal the flour to obtain rich dough. This dough would be very difficult but not impossible to work with.

Pate Sucre is a sweet version of this pastry and sugar is creamed with butter before the flour and the moisture is added. The ratio of sugar fat and flour is 1:2:4. Various sweet and savoury products are made with short crust pastry. It forms the base of several pies, tarts, flans and also products like cheese straws and turnovers. A related type is the sweetened sweet crust pastry, also known as *pâte sucrée*, in which sugar and egg yolks have been added (rather than water) to bind the pastry.

Few precautions must be taken when making short crust pastry. It is important not to work the dough too much as it will get tough due to the development of gluten. This can also happen when scrapings and trimmings are added to the dough and re –worked. The use of too much flour for dusting will also alter the ratio of the mixture and cause toughening as the extra flour proteins – *glutenin* and *gliadin* – does not have a coating of fat around it, and thus come together to form gluten.

Types of short crust pastries:

1. ***Pâte à foncer*** is French shortcrust pastry that includes egg. Egg and butter are worked together with a small quantity of sugar and salt before the flour is drawn into the mixture and cold water added to bind it.

2. ***Pâte brisée*** is similar to pâte à foncer, but is lighter and more delicate due to an increased quantity of butter – up to three –fifths the quantity of flour. Very often is made with no sugar, as a savoury crust for pies.

3. ***Pâte sucrée*** (sweetcrust pastry, sweet dough, or sweet paste) is made with more sugar, which sweetens the mix and impedes the gluten strands, creating a pastry that breaks up easily in the mouth. An alternative is gluten–free pastry.

4. ***Pâte sablée*** has the same ingredients as pâte sucrée, but the butter is creamed with the sugar and the eggs before the flour is folded in. This mixes the butter more evenly, which makes the dough puff much less, creating a more "snappy" and dry pastry, instead of the crumbly texture of the previous doughs. Sablée works better for sweet tarts, tea biscuits, and piped shapes than other short doughs, as they hold their shape much more efficiently, and are the basis for gingerbread and sandwich biscuits. No water is needed, neither is the dough particularly temperature –sensitive.

Qualities of Short Dough:

- A short dough should be non –elastic and somewhat brittle, easily breaking apart when pulled. In many cases it may only just come together when mixed, and may be sticky or have a crumbly texture like sand.
- The baked products that it produces are typically rich and crumbly, with a distinct tenderness much desired in sweet tarts, biscuits or cookies.
- The qualities produced by a short dough can be best appreciated by comparing them to products made from a non –short, or "hard" dough.
- The basic ingredients for bread are flour, water, salt and leaven, and so most often it is made from a dough containing no added fat.

- The tough, chewy nature of bread can therefore be seen as at the opposite end of the spectrum to a sweet, tender short dough.

Recipe:

Ingredients –

- Unsalted butter –280gm, softened to room temperature
- Granulated sugar – ½ cup plus 2 tbsp
- Egg –1no
- Vanilla – ½ tsp
- All purpose flour3 cups
- Salt – ½ tsp

Method

- Cream butter and sugar just until combined and slightly aerated.
- Add the egg and vanilla, mix to combine and scrape down the bowl and beater.
- Add flour and salt and mix until the dough just begins to come together.
- Remove from the mixer and knead into a ball.
- Flatten the ball to a disc, wrap in plastic and refrigerate for 1 – 2 hours before using.
- Use as required for tarts, pies, biscuits or cookies.

CHAPTER TEN

PUFF PASTRIES

Puff pastry is one of the most remarkable products of the bakeshop. Although it includes no added leavening agent, it can rise to eight times its original thickness when baked. Puff pastry is rolled –in dough, like Danish and croissant doughs. This means that it is made up of many layers of fat sandwiched between layers of dough. Puff pastry can be made as up to thousand layers or more. The whole purpose of rolling and folding is to build up a layered structure of alternating layers of dough and fat. This process is known as *lamination*. Unlike Danish dough, however, puff pastry contains no yeast. Steam, created when the moisture in the dough is heated, is responsible for the spectacular rising power of puff pastry. As with so many other products, there are nearly as many versions of puff pastry as there are bakers. Both formulas and rolling –in techniques vary.

INGREDIENTS

Refined Flour – The flour that is used in making of puff pastry should be strong, with good quality gluten. A good patent flour or one of medium gluten strength 13% flour is a structure builder and because of its gluten – forming ability, can dictate the lift. Too soft a flour will result in a softer dough. The dough will be easier to handle but final volume and flake will be sacrificed. It the flour is too strong then the dough will be tough to handle and the final product may suffer from shrinkage.

Water – It is a rule of thumb that the consistency of the dough should match the consistency of the roll in fat. If the dough is too soft then the layers may be ruptured by the hard fat. If the dough is firm, it will be difficult to roll out. The product may shrink and fat may leak out. Water also serves as temperature control i.e. it should be cold to maintain firmness of fat.

Salt – Salt enhances flavor and also has a toughening effect on the gluten structure.

Acid – The addition of an acid improves sheeting ability by lowering the pH and mellowing the gluten. It has no effect on the leavening action. A weak acid such as lemon juice is added. This provides greater extensibility to the gluten.

Puff Pastry Shortening –Butter is the preferred fat for rolling in because of its flavor and melt –in the mouth quality. Special puff pastry shortening like semi solid lard or margarine is also available. Every shortening performs a different role. They are added to the dough to modify the dough itself and as a layering medium to assist in the raising of the puff pastry during baking. These shortenings are easier to work because they are not as hard when refrigerated and because they don't soften and melt at warm temperatures as easily as butter does. They are firm and waxy in nature and are exclusively used to make puffs. They are also less expensive than butter. Because of their nature, they can be rolled out in smooth continuous sheets between the dough layers. Their melting point between $43^0C - 50^0C$ will produce excellent results, but should be high enough to with stand frictional heat to which they are subjected during sheeting and folding operation. However, it can be unpleasant to eat because it tends to congeal and coat the inside of the mouth.

Puff Pastry Types: There are two types of puff pastry – Full and Three Quarter. There are three well –known methods of manufacture – English, French and Scotch. The differences in these types are in the fat contents and in the number of rolls and folds given. Full puff pastry contains flour and fat in equal ratio. While ¾ pastry contains ¾ of fat to each kilogram of flour.

The English method (Three Fold) – (Flaky): Sieve the flour; rub in 20 gms of butter or margarine. Make a bay or well, add salt and acid and make a dough and allow it to rest. Cream the margarine into a homogenous mass. The dough then rolled into a rectangle about 18" x 6", the margarine is divided into approx. 3 parts. The first part is evenly distributed to cover 2/3rd of the rolled out dough. The flap of the dough containing no margarine is folded over to cover half of the treated area and then folded over to again cover the last portion. The pastry is given a half turn so that the open ends are parallel to the rolling pin. This process is repeated twice so as to finish all the margarine. Lastly one blindfold is given. The pastry is covered with a damp cloth and allowed to recover from the manipulation for about 30 minutes after each rolling. (7 – 9 layers).

French method – (Continental Book Fold): The dough is the same fashion as for the English method. The initial rolling out of the dough is different for it is rolled out to the shape of an open envelope with the four angles slightly thinner than the center. The chilled margarine/

butter is placed in the center of the rolled out square and the envelope is closed by bringing the four angles to the center. After proper relaxation of the dough, it is turned upside down and sheeted into a rectangular shape and folded in a book fold.

Scotch Method – (Blitz): This is the quickest way of making puff pastry. The word is derived from the German word "Blitzen" meaning lightening. In this method the chilled margarine is mixed into the sieved flour in pieces about the size walnuts. The folding process is a three fold followed by 3 – Four folds, all of which is accomplished in 25 min.

Baking : Puff pastry obtains its lifting power through the sealing of moisture in the dough, as heat penetrates the product, the layers of shortening melt and the water in the dough vaporizes and causes the layers to expand. The shortening also helps by holding in these vapors. The gluten in the dough expands with the pressure of the steam and holds the steam in. The shortening melts and penetrates the layers of the dough, making it flaky and tender. The starch then gelatinizes and the proteins coagulate forming a rigid mass. The structure remains firm and flaky.

Oven Temperature : Proper oven temperature is important. A temperature of 204^0C – 218^0C with an even steady heat is very important. Too low a temperature allows shortening to weep between the layers of dough resulting in poor quality and low volume. Too high a temperature prematurely seals the piece and results in low volume and raw centers.

Washing: Puff pastry pieces are generally washed with an egg wash. Care should be taken to prevent the wash from running down the sides of the pieces while brushing the top. The eggs will coagulate with the heat of the oven, seal the sides and prevent the pastry from rising evenly. (Poor Volume).

Guidelines for makeup and baking of puff dough products:

- Dough should be cool and firm when it is rolled and cut. If it is too soft, layers may stick together at the cuts, preventing proper rising.
- Cut with straight, firm, even cuts. Use a sharp cutting tool.
- Avoid touching the cut edges with the fingers, or layers may stick together.
- For best rising, place the units upside down on baking sheets. Even sharp cutting tools may press the top layers of dough together. Baking upside down puts the stuck –together layers at the bottom.
- Avoid letting egg wash run down the edges. Egg wash can cause the layers to stick together at the edges.
- Rest made –up products for 30 minutes or more in a cool place or in the refrigerator before baking. This relaxes the gluten and reduces shrinkage.
- Trimmings may be pressed together, keeping the layers in the same direction. After being rolled out and given a three –fold, they may be used again, although they will not rise as high.
- Baking temperatures of 400° to 425°F (200° to 220°C) are best for most puff dough products. Cooler temperatures will not create enough steam in the products to leaven them well. Higher temperatures will set the crust too quickly.

Recipe Ingredients –

- Refined flour –1 ½ cups
- Butter –1 cup
- Salt –1 pinch
- Water – ½ cup

Method –

- On a surface place flour and salt. Slowly pour in water Mix till you get a smooth dough. Put in the refrigerator for 1 or 2 hours.
- In the meantime, take the butter and roll it out with some flour into a rectangular shape. Put in the
- refrigerator for about 30 minutes.
- Take the dough out of the fridge, roll it out in a rectangular shape.
- On top of the dough place the butter. Fold one side. Then the other. Refrigerate for 20 minutes.
- Roll the dough out into a rectangular shape
- Fold it again, refrigerate for 30 minutes. Repeat the process from 3 to 6 times
- Bake at the desired temperature.

Common Problems with Puff Pastries and their reasons:

1. Puff dough has white spots or ice crystals on it: Freezing and thawing many times
2. Puff dough stick to the table: Work table rough. Dough left out on the table for a long time.
3. Puff dough sheets and squares crack when handling: Dough was not thawed enough to handle. Dough had dried out while working with it.
4. Puff dough tear while working: Dough is rolled too thin.
5. Fat Runs Out: Dough not folded enough. Oven is too cold. Warm pans are used. Melting point of fat is too low.
6. Puff is Hard and Tough: Too much water has been added to the flour but not enough fat. Handling the dough too much. Inferior quality flour.
7. Puff is Soggy in the Middle: Undercooked. Very high oven temperature.
8. Edges fell over while baking: Crust is too thick and falls over because of its own weight. Too high a proportion of fat in the recipe. Under mixing. Placing warm dough in the over to bake before it has been chilled will also contribute to this problem.
9. Loss of sweetness, open texture and lack of crust color: Proofed too long. Excessive retarding time.
10. Blisters on baked product: Too much humidity

CHAPTER ELEVEN

ECLAIRS AND CREAM PUFFS

An éclair is an oblong pastry made with choux dough filled with a pastry cream or custard and topped with chocolate icing or dipped in fondant icing. The word comes from the French éclair, meaning "flash of lightning", so named because it is eaten quickly (in a flash).The dough, which is the same as that used for profiterole, is typically piped into an oblong shape with a pastry bag and baked until it is crisp and hollow inside.

The word "éclair" made its appearance in the 1860s, describing the pastry previously called petite duchesse in France. It may have been created by French chef Antonin Carême, who is responsible for other desserts including the Charlotte and Napolean cake. Its first print reference in English was in an article in Vanity Fair in 1861, and then in Boston Cooking School Cook Book in 1884. The eclair is making a resurgence in popularity and can now be seen filled with trendy fillings such as matcha tea or mocha cream filling. The tops of the pastry may now be decorated with fresh fruit and fanciful fruit glazes. Frozen eclairs are also to be found with ice cream fillings.

A cream puff (US), profiterole (English) or chou à la crème (French) is a filled French choux pastry ball with a typically sweet and moist filling of whipped cream, custard, pastry cream, or ice cream. The puffs may be decorated or left plain or garnished with chocolate sauce, caramel, or a dusting of powdered sugar.

The choux pastry (pâte à choux) is a key component of the éclair or cream puff or profiteroles, and gougères. This pastry rises only from the action of steam. It doesn't use any yeast, baking soda, or baking powder. This makes the éclairs different from long – shaped doughnuts such as the Long John, which are made with doughnut pastry that uses another leavening. Choux pastry is made by heating milk, water, sugar, salt, and butter to a boil, stirring in bread flour to incorporate it, allowing it to cool a little, then adding eggs. Choux pastry dough is piped through a pastry bag or dropped with a pair of spoons into small balls and baked to form largely hollow puffs. The dough is then baked at a high heat to generate the steam and get the dough to rise. Then the oven temperature is lowered to complete baking and brown the pastry.

The result is an airy, almost hollow shell that is crisp enough on top to be iced. After cooling, it is ready to be filled with a variety of fillings as desired. A thicker filling is best to prevent the bottom of the pastry from getting soggy. After cooling, the baked éclairs and profiteroles are injected with filling using a pastry bag and narrow piping tip, or by slicing off the top, filling them, and reassembling. For sweet profiteroles, additional glazes or decorations may then be added. Pastry cream is often the filling. It is thick custard made with egg yolks, milk, sugar, cornstarch, and may include butter. The icing should be one that hardens, such as fondant or ganache. This allows the éclair to be handled easier. A second flavor of icing may be piped on top for decoration and added taste.

Cream puffs, Eclairs and gougères can be stored in an airtight container at room temperature for up to two days, or freeze them for up to six weeks in a ziptop freezer bag. The exact procedure for making éclair paste is detailed in the formula that follows. In general, the method consists of these steps:

- Bring the liquid, fat, salt, and sugar (if used) to a boil. The liquid must be boiling rapidly so the fat is dispersed in the liquid, not just floating on top.
- If this is not done, the fat will not be as well incorporated into the paste, and some of it may run out during baking.
- Add the flour all at once and stir until the paste forms a ball and pulls away from the sides of the pan.
- Remove the paste from the heat and let it cool to 140°F (60°C).If the paste is not cooled slightly, it will cook the eggs when they are added.
- Beat in the eggs a little at a time. Completely mix in each addition of eggs before adding more. If the eggs are added too quickly, it will be difficult to get a smooth batter.
- The paste is now ready to use.

Recipe of Choux paste

Ingredients –

- Butter – ½ cup

- Water –1 cup
- All –purpose flour –1 cup
- Salt –¼ tsp
- Eggs – 4 large

Method –

1. Combine the liquid, butter, and salt in a heavy saucepan or kettle. Bring the mixture to a full, rolling boil.
2. Remove the pan from the heat and add the flour all at once. Stir quickly.
3. Return the pan to moderate heat and stir vigorously until the dough forms a ball and pulls away from the sides of the pan.
4. Transfer the dough to the bowl of a mixer. If you wish to mix it by hand, leave it in the saucepan.
5. With the paddle attachment, mix at low speed until the dough has cooled slightly. It should be about 140°F (60°C), which is still very warm, but not too hot to touch.
6. At medium speed, beat in the eggs a little at a time. Add no more than a quarter of the eggs at once, and wait until they are completely absorbed before adding more. When all the eggs are absorbed, the paste is ready to use.

Recipe of éclairs Ingredients –

- Choux paste – 400 gms

Fillings and Icings

- Package instant vanilla pudding mix –150 gm
- Cold milk – 2 ½ cups
- Heavy cream –1 cup
- Confectioners' sugar –¼ cup
- Vanilla extract –1 tsp
- Semisweet chocolate –100 gm
- Butter –2 tbsp
- Confectioners' sugar –1 cup
- Vanilla extract –1 tsp
- Hot water –3 tbsp

Method –

- Preheat oven to 450^0F (230^0C). Grease a cookie sheet.
- With a spoon or a pastry bag fitted with a No. 10, or larger, tip, spoon or pipe choux paste onto cookie sheet in 1 ½ x 4 inch strips.
- Bake 15 minutes in the preheated oven, then reduce heat to 325^0F (165^0C) and bake 20 minutes more, until hollow sounding when lightly tapped on the bottom. Cool completely on a wire rack.
- For the filling, combine pudding mix and milk in medium bowl according to package directions. In a separate bowl, beat the cream with an electric mixer until soft peaks form. Beat in ¼ cup confectioners' sugar and 1 tsp vanilla. Fold whipped cream into pudding. Cut tops off of cooled pastry shells with a sharp knife. Fill shells with pudding mixture and replace tops.

- For the icing, melt the chocolate and 2 tbsps butter in a medium saucepan over low heat. Stir in 1 cup confectioners' sugar and 1 tsp vanilla. Stir in hot water, one tbsp at a time, until icing is smooth and has reached desired consistency. Remove from heat, cool slightly, and drizzle over filled éclairs. Refrigerate until serving.

Recipe of Cream puff or Profiteroles
Ingredients –

- Choux paste – 400 gms

For chocolate filling:

- White chocolate –125 gm chopped
- Cream –60 ml
- Butter –50 gm
- Yolks –2 egg
- Rum –to taste

For chocolate cream topping:

- Water –275 ml
- Sugar –275 gm
- Cocoa powder –1 tbsp
- Dark chocolate –75 gm chopped
- Cream –125 ml

- Butter −2 tbsp

Method –

- Preheat oven to 450^{0}F (230^{0}C). Grease a cookie sheet.
- With a pastry bag fitted with a No. 10, or larger tip, pipe choux paste onto cookie sheet into small domes.
- Bake 15 minutes in the preheated oven, then reduce heat to 325^{0}F (165^{0}C) and bake 20 minutes more, until hollow sounding when lightly tapped on the bottom.
- After baking, pierce each profiterole to allow steam to escape. Return pastry to a low oven to dry out.
- Take out and cool completely on a wire rack.

For the filling:

- Melt white chocolate with the cream and butter. Cool.
- Stir in yolks add rum mix by cut and fold method.
- Cut the profiteroles in half, fill them with the sweetened cream and pile them up on a plate.

For the topping sauce:

- Prepare sugar syrup with water, sugar, add dark chocolate, cocoa powder, cook till thick.
- Cool and then add cream and butter
- Drizzle or layer the Profiteroles on top. And serve.
-

Tips to ensure success: Éclairs and Profiteroles might look tricky and fancy, but they are actually very straightforward to make if you follow just 3 key tips:

- Cool dough before adding eggs – this is the key to ensure the heat from the dough doesn't cook the eggs and so they incorporate properly when mixed together. The egg is the key to making the Choux pastry rise and become hollow.
- Mix eggs in thoroughly – the dough will look like it splits when you start mixing the eggs in, but persist! The batter will come together – it needs to be smooth;
- Don't pierce until crispy – A key step is to remove the profiteroles partway through baking to pierce a hole in them, and then return into the oven. This is to make them dry out and cook inside so they hold their shape (and so it's not raw batter inside).

Common problems with Éclairs and Cream puffs

1. Not rising or flattened: Oven temperature less. Too much eggs. Excess water. Excess butter.
2. Getting soggy: Pastry not pierced, to allow the trapped air to escape. Not dried in oven. Not rested on wire mesh. Gone old so the crust becomes soft from the moisture inside.
3. Collapsed: High heat. Too much fat. Water and butter mixture not boiling while added to the flour. Allow enough space between puffs, to let the steam escape when they expand. Oven door opened in the middle of baking.
4. Uneven and large cracks: Sugar and/or salt are not dissolved completely. Water loss during prolonged

boiling of water sugar and butter. Flour not shifted. Dough is beaten for too long resulting in separation of fat. Less salt added.

CHAPTER TWELVE

CREAM CHEESE DOUGH

Cream cheese is an American invention developed in 1872 in New York State. It is a soft cow's –milk, mild tangy tasting fresh cheese with a high fat content (approx 35%), spreadable texture and creamy white in colour.Cream cheese is categorized as a fresh cheese since it is unaged. As a result, it has ashort shelf life, once opened. It is available in various sized solid white blocks or whipped and flavored. Cream cheese should be gently softened before blending them into fillings, icings and batters. Blend the cheese on low speed with a paddle to soften and remove lumps before adding sugar, eggs or other liquid ingredient.

Cream cheese is one of the most popular soft cheese products in North America. Its soft creamy texture gives richness to cheesecake, frosting, bagel –toppers, and dips and makes wonderfully light and flaky pastry crusts. It is used as a popular spread for bagels and toast, in cheesecakes, pastry fillings and icings. Cream cheese is sometimes used in place of or with butter (typically two parts cream cheese to one part butter) when making cakes or cookies, and cream cheese frosting.

Similar to American, another important cream cheese is French *Neufchâtel*, which has less fat than regular cream cheese, but it also has more moisture. Cream cheese is sold in large blocks, tubs, or smaller packages.

Cream cheese is categorized as a fresh cheese since it is unaged. As a result, it has a short shelf life, once opened. At room temperature, cream cheese spreads easily and has a smooth and creamy texture. It can be rolled beautifully without splitting or crumbling. It is sold in foil –wrapped blocks or in a soft –spread form which has air whipped in to make it spreadable right from the refrigerator.

Recipe of Cream cheese dough Ingredients –

- All –purpose flour –2 ¾ cups (380gm)
- Granulated sugar –1 tbsp (14gm)
- Table salt –1 tsp
- Cream cheese, cut into 1" chunks – ½ cup (120gm)
- Unsalted butter, cold and cut into 1" chunks –1 stick (80gm)
- Heavy whipping cream – ¼ cup (60ml)
- Cold water – ¼ cup (60 ml)
-

Method –

- Whisk together the flour, sugar and salt in a mixing bowl.

- Toss in the cream cheese. Using your fingers, mix the cream cheese into the flour until it resembles coarse corn meal.
- Toss the butter into the flour and use your fingers to work it in. Allow the flakes to break up into slightly smaller pieces. Work quickly so the butter doesn't get warm. Don't break the butter down completely. There should be some large flakes remaining.
- Pour the cream and water onto the flour all at once and toss to combine. Gently work the dough just until it comes together. Form the dough into a rectangle or square, wrap and refrigerate for at least 2 – 3 hours, or make it the day before and let it rest overnight.
- The dough can be frozen for up to 3 months.

Cream cheese dough products:

- Cheesecake
- Rugelach
- Blue cheese tart
- Cream Cheese Pastry

Recipe of Cheese cake

Ingredients –

- Cream cheese – 4500 gm
- Sugar –1575 gm
- Cornstarch – 90 gm
- Lemon zest, grated –15 gm

- Vanilla extract – 30 gm
- Salt – 45 gm
- Eggs – 900 gm
- Egg yolks – 340 gm
- Heavy cream – 450 gm
- Milk – 225 gm
- Lemon juice – 60 gm
- Cream cheese dough – as required

Method –Cheesecake may be baked with or without a water bath. Baking in a water bath results in cakes with browned tops and unbrowned sides. Baking without a water bath results in browned sides and a lighter top.

- Prepare the pans by lining the bottoms with either a very thin layer of cream cheese dough. Prebake the short dough until it begins to turn golden.
- Put the cream cheese in the mixing bowl and, with the paddle attachment, mix at low speed until smooth and lump free.
- Add the sugar, cornstarch, lemon zest, vanilla, and salt. Blend in until smooth and uniform, but do not whip. Scrape down the sides of the bowl and the beater.
- Add the eggs and egg yolks, a little at a time, blending them in thoroughly after each addition. Scrape down the bowl again to make sure the mixture is well blended.
- With the machine running at low speed, gradually add the cream, milk, and lemon juice.
- Fill the prepared pans. Scale as follows:

  - 10" pans—2050 gm
  - 9" pans—1600 gm
  - 8" pans—1350 gm

- To bake without a water bath, place the filled pans on sheet pans and set them in an oven preheated to 200°C. After 10 minutes, turn the oven down to 105°C and continue baking until the mixture is set, about 1–1 ½ hours, depending on the size of the cake.
- To bake with a water bath, set the filled pans inside another, larger pan. Fill the outer pan with water and bake at 175°C until set.
- Cool the cakes completely before removing from pans. To unmold a cake from a pan without removable sides, sprinkle the top of the cake with granulated sugar.
- Invert the cake onto a cardboard cake circle, then immediately place another circle over the bottom and turn it right –side up.

Recipe of Rugelach Ingredients –

- Light brown sugar – ¼ cup
- Ground cinnamon –1 ½tsps
- Raisins – ¾ cup
- Walnuts, finely chopped –1 cup
- Apricot preserves, pureed in a food processor – ½ cup For egg wash
- Egg beaten –1
- milk –1 tbsp
- Cream cheese dough – as required

Method –

- To make the filling, combine 6 tbsps of granulated suar, the brown sugar, ½tsp cinnamon, the raisins, and walnuts.

- On a well – floured board, each ball roll of dough into a 9–inch circle.
- Spread the dough with 2 tbsps apricot preserves and sprinkle with ½ cup of the filling.
- Press the filling lightly into the dough. Cut the circle into 12 equal wedges.
- Starting with the wide edge, roll up each wedge. wide edge, roll up each wedge.
- Place the cookies, points tuckedtucked under, on a baking sheet lined with parchment paper.
- Chill for 30 minutes.

- Preheat the oven to 350 degrees F.
- Brush each cookie with the egg wash.
- Combine 3 tbsps granulated sugar and 1 tsp cinnamon and sprinkle on the cookies.
- Bake for 15 to 20 minutes, until lightly br wned. Remove to a wire rack and let cool.

CHAPTER THIRTEEN

ICINGS AND WHIPPED CREAM TOPPINGS

These are common name of prepared confections that are used to cover and decorate cakes. When they are placed in between two or more layers they are referred as fillings.

Icings: Icing, also known as frosting, is a sweet decorative creamy glaze coating used as a filling between the layers or as a coating over the top and sides of a cake. It is used to add flavor and to improve a cake's appearance. Icing can also extend a cake's shelf life by forming a protective coating. There are seven general types of icing: buttercream, foam, fudge, fondant, glaze, royal icing and ganache. Each type can be produced with a number of formulas and in a range of flavorings. Because icing is integral to the flavor and appearance of many cakes, it should be made carefully using high –quality ingredients and natural flavors and colors. A good icing is smooth; it is never grainy or lumpy. It should complement the flavor and texture of the cake without overpowering it. A basic icing is called a glacé, containing powdered sugar (also known as icing sugar or confectioners' sugar) and water. This can be flavored and colored as desired, for example, by using lemon juice in place of the water.

Icings have three main functions –

- They improve the keeping qualities of the cake by forming protective coatings around it.
- They contribute flavour and richness
- They improve appearance.

Types of Icing –

There are six basic types of icings and other cake coatings

- Fondant
- Buttercreams
- Foam type icings
- Fudge type Icings
- Flat type Icings
- Royal or decorator's icing

Others

- Glazes
- Rolled coatings

Fondant

Fondant is sugar syrup that is crystallized to a smooth creamy white mass. When applied it sets up into a shiny, non –sticky coating.

Fondant is prepared by dissolving 500gms of granulated or cube sugar in 150 ml of water and 15 ml of glucose and then allowed to boil gradually till it reaches the soft ball stage 112 –116°C (234 –240°F) which may be tested by dropping a little syrup in iced water where it will from a ball under water but lose its shape immediately when it is exposed to air. The syrup must be cooled immediately and the air bubbles then subside.

The syrup is, then, poured out into a cold surface and worked first with a spatula until it turns from a clear liquid to a white crumbly solid. It is then kneaded by hand until smooth and finished by being left to ripen in a cool place for at least 12 hours.

The object is to produce minute crystals in a super saturated solution of sugar giving a creamy texture to the finished product.

Uses –

- For first coating on fruit cakes before applying Royal icing.
- For dipping fresh fruits to make confections for immediate consumption.
- For casting into moulds.
- Pastel coloured icing for cakes

Butter Cream Icings or Crème Au Beurre

Butter cream icings are light smooth mixtures of fat and icing sugar which are creamed together to the desired consistency and lightness. They may also contain eggs to increase their smoothness or lightness. This icing is very popular and is used for covering many kinds of cake. They are easily flavoured and coloured to suit a variety of purposes.

There are four types of basic kinds of butter cream:

a. **Simple butter cream**, also called American buttercream are made by creaming together fat and powdered sugar to the desired consistency, a small quantity of egg white may be whipped in to obtain the desired lightness.Note that cream cheese frosting is merely simple buttercream which uses cream cheese instead of butter as the fat.

b. **Decorators butter cream** is a simple butter cream used for making flowers and other cake decorations. Because butter tends to melt at room temperature (or at least become very soft), buttercream frosting is not ideal for producing the decorative flowers and curlicues you see on fancy wedding cakes. The solution is to so −called decorator's buttercream, which—instead of butter—is made with vegetable shortening. It is creamed only a little, because if too much air is incorporated, it lacks in lightness, it makes up for in stability, making it ideal for producing those decorative flourishes.

c. **Meringue butter creams**, sometimes called Swiss or Italian meringue buttercream, this variation is made by beating a hot syrup of sugar and water into a basic egg white foam, then whipping softened butter into the resulting meringue to make the frosting. Heating the meringue gives it extra stability, which means this frosting is extremely light and airy.

d. **French butter creams**, is probably the richest buttercream and yet it's also extremely light in texture.

It's made by adding boiling syrup into beaten egg yolks and then whipping into a foamy consistency, to which softened butter is then added and beaten some more until light and creamy. Unsalted butter is the preferred fat for butter creams because of its flavour and melt in the mouth quality.

e. **Pastry –Cream Butter cream**, also known as German buttercream, this variation is made by combining pastry cream (which is custard with some sort of added starch, such as flour or cornstarch) with butter, and possibly additional confectioner's sugar.

Recipe for Butter icing

1. Beat 125 gms. of butter add 125 gms. of icing sugar with 30 gm of milk and flavouring. Beat until creamy and smooth.
2. Butter cream or crème au beurre –Place 2 egg whites and 125gm of icing sugar in a mixing bowl and whisk until mixture holds shape. Cool slightly. Cream 125 gm butter until soft then beat in the meringue mixture a little at a time. Flavour or colour as desired.

Foam Type Icing

They are also known as boiled icings. They are simple meringues made with boiling syrup and may also contain gelatin as a stabilizer. Foam type icings should be applied thickly to cakes and left in peaks and swirls. These icings are not stable and should be used they day they are prepared.

Flat Icings

These icings are also known as water icings and are mixtures of confectioner's sugar, water, sometimes corn syrup and flavouring. They are used for coffee cakes, Danish party and sweet rolls. They are a simple mixture consisting of five pounds of powdered sugar 300ml water, 200 ml corn syrup and flavouring as desired. Egg white may also be added to lighten the frosting.

Fudge Type Icing

Fudge type icings are rich cooked icings. They are heavy and thick and they may be flavoured by a variety of ingredients. They are used on cup cakes, layer cakes, loaf cakes, sheet cakes, etc. To store fudge icings they must be properly covered with cling film and then kept in an airtight container in the refrigerator. To use stored fudge icing, warm in a double boiler until it is soft enough to spread. They are stable frostings which hold their shape well on cakes and cup cakes.

Chocolate Fudge Frosting

- Sugar – 450 gms
- Glucose or corn syrup – 150 gms
- Water – 120 ml
- Butter – 150 gms

- Sugar powder – 375 gms
- Cocoa powder – 175 gms
- Vanilla essence – to taste

Method –

- Combine granulated sugar, glucose and water and boil till 116°C.
- Sift powdered sugar and cocoa together, cream sugar/cocoa with butter till light and fluffy and gradually add syrup and essence and blend well.
- Use immediately while still warm and spreadable.

Royal Icing

This icing is the traditional covering for Christmas and wedding cakes, and is made from icing sugar beaten with egg whites and lemon juice; a tsp of glycerin may be added. In the hands of a skilled confectioner this can be used to produce perfectly flat smooth surfaces or piped into intricate borders, patterns or trellis work, which are very fragile but very hard when set. It is always applied over a layer of marzipan or fondant.

Recipe for royal icing for 6 inch round or 5 inch square cakes –

- Egg whites –2. No.
- Icing Sugar –500 gms

- Lemon juice –1 tsp
- Glycerine –1 tsp
- Cream of tartar –2.5 gms

Method –

- Beat the egg whites with a fork until frothy
- Gradually beat in ½ the icing sugar, using a wooden spoon (+ Lemon juice and cream of tartar)
- Beat in the remaining icing sugar with the glycerin
- Beat thoroughly until smooth and white, and having a consistency that stands in soft peaks.
- Add coloring if required.
- Cover the bowl with a damp cloth and leave it to stand for several hours to allow bubbles to escape. Before using stir well with wooden spoon but do not over beat.

Other Icings similar to Royal Icing are –

Sugar paste or Moulded Icing: Beat one egg white and 15 ml glucose gradually adding 500gm icing sugar to form a still paste. Turn unto a surface sprinkled with corn flour and knead until smooth. Wrap in cling film and keep and keep in a plastic bag to prevent it from drying, will keep refrigerated for 6 weeks. This quantity is sufficient to cover 8 inch round cake.

Satin Icing: Boil together 50 gms of butter + lemon juice +dissolved 250 gm of icing sugar and cook for 2 min. Remove from heat and beat in another 250 gm of icing sugar till stiff. Gradually mix in another 175 gm of icing sugar and knead until smooth preserve as above.

Glazes or Glace: Glazes are thin glossy transparent coatings that give shine to baked products and help prevent drying. The simplest mixture for this purpose is syrup made from 250 gms of icing sugar in 30 ml of water or milk. They are brushed over small cakes or poured to give a smooth finish. The glaze recipes are of two types: chocolate and gelatin–based. Chocolate glazes are usually melted chocolate containing additional fats or liquids, or both. They are applied warm and set up to form a thin, shiny coating. Gelatin based glazes, which include many fruit glazes, are usually applied only to the tops of cakes and charlottes made in ring molds. Ganache may also be considered as an icing.

Ganache: A flavoured cream made with chocolate and fresh cream, sometimes with butter added. It may be used as a sauce, or to glaze a cake or it may be whipped and used a filling and/or icing. Ganache can also be made of stiffer consistency, chilled and rolled into truffles or as topping for petit fours. It was created in Paris round about 1850

Method –Bring 100 ml of double cream to the boil. Remove from heat and add 225 gms of plain unsweetened chocolate broken into even squares. Stir until the chocolate has melted and is thoroughly combined with cream. Leave until cool but not set then whip until pale, thick and light or before whipping it may be poured over cakes as chocolate icing.

Toppings are anything that is used to cover a cake or a pastry and it may be fruits, jam, nuts etc. and Icings are that part of toppings which are sweet coatings that may be applied to cakes and pastries.

Rolled Coatings : The three commonly used rolled cake coatings are rolled fondant, marzipan, and modeling chocolate. Rather than being applied by spreading or pouring like the other products discussed, these are rolled into thin sheets, using a rolling pin, and draped over the cake to cover it. To ensure the coating adheres to the cake, the cake is first brushed with apricot glaze or a similar product, or iced with a thin layer of buttercream before the rolled coating is applied.

Rolled fondant is a dough like product consisting primarily of confectioner's sugar combined with small quantities of glucose, water, gelatin, and other ingredients to give it the proper consistency. It is firm and stiff enough to be kneaded, and pliable enough to be rolled out in thin sheets. Like poured fondant, it is almost always purchased ready prepared.

Marzipan is a paste made of ground almonds and sugar.

Modeling chocolate is a stiff paste made of melted chocolate and corn syrup.

Rules for selection of icing

- The flavour texture and colour of icing must be compatible with the cake.
- In general use heavy frosting with heavy cakes and light frosting with light cakes.

e.g. Angel food cakes with simple flat icings. High ratio cakes with butter cream or fudge type icings. Genoese sponge with French or meringue type icing.

- Use the best quality flavourings and use them sparingly.
- The flavour of the frosting should not be stronger than the cake.

- Use colour sparingly, light pastel shades are more appetizing than loud colours.

Whipped cream topping/frosting: Whipped cream frostings is smooth and satiny texture which consist of whipped cream, powdered sugar, and flavorings such as vanilla, pineapple, strawberry etc. The commonly whipped cream is Chantilly cream which has vanilla as flavouring agent. As with butter cream, the cornstarch in the powdered sugar helps stabilize the frosting. It is used as a filling for cakes, as a frosting, one can pipe it, or it can be used simply as an accompaniment to a slice of pie, a bowl of fresh fruit, or to garnish a pudding.

Preparation of whipped cream : While making whipped cream frosting it is mandatory to the cream, the bowl, and the wire whisk very cold, as this will help the cream reach its maximum volume when whipped. It is best to use a metal bowl and place it in the freezer, along with the wire whisk, for at least 15 minutes. Always use heavy cream, also known as heavy "whipping" cream. This is cream with a butterfat content of between 35 – 40%, which means it will double in volume and reach stiff peaks when beaten. When beating the cream, add it to the cold mixer bowl, along with the vanilla and sugar. Start the mixer at low speed and gradually increase the speed to high. Depending on what you are using the cream for, beat just until soft or stiff peaks form. Cream beaten longer turns into butter, so necessary precaution to be taken. If you do accidentally over beat, just add a little more cream and beat until soft or stiff peaks form. To stabilize the cream so it will not separate when stored, take about 1 tsp unflavored gelatin and sprinkle it over 1 tbsp cold water. Let it stand about 5 –10 minutes or until it has softened and swelled (bloom). Then heat it gently (I do this in the microwave in 5 second intervals) to dissolve the gelatin. Then whisk it into the softly whipped cream.

Recipe Ingredients –

- Heavy whipping cream –1 cup
- Powdered sugar – ½ cup

Method –

- Place the mixing bowl and whisk attachment in the freezer for 5 to 10 minutes to chill.
- Prepare the whipped cream. Pour the heavy cream into the chilled bowl and use an electric or stand mixer to beat the heavy cream on medium –high speed until the cream starts to thicken.
- Slowly add the powdered sugar and continue beating on high speed until stiff peaks form.

CHAPTER FOURTEEN

CAKES AND CAKE SPECIALTIES

Cakes have their part to play in ancient beliefs and superstitions, some which still carries on to modern times. In olden times, people used cakes as offerings to their gods and spirits around the world. The Chinese celebrate Harvest Moon festival and have moon cakes to honour their moon goddess. This tradition continues up to today. Russians have sun cakes called blini which are thin pancakes to pay their respect to a deity called Maslenitsa. Ancient Celts rolled cakes down a hill during the Beltane festival held on the first day of spring to imitate solar movement. With such a rich history and connection of humans with cake, it is no wonder that they remain such an important part of our lives.

Why are cakes round? Although these days we have a variety of shapes from heart –shaped to cartoon characters, animals, castles and even R –rated shapes if you are so inclined, cakes are traditionally round. This symbolizes the cyclical nature of life, the sun and the moon, which is probably the reason why we have cakes during important events; highlighting that we are embarking on a new journey in our life –span. Ancient breads were also round, typically fashioned into round balls and baked in shallow pans. In the 17th century, cake hoops made from metal or wood were increasingly used.

When did cakes become easier to make? The invention of baking soda and baking powder during the Industrial Revolution increased the popularity of baking cakes due to the ease provided to the masses. Ovens were beginning to have more temperature controlled settings which meant people could leave their cakes to bake without labouring and watching over them constantly. Railroads also made ingredients readily available and cheaper.

So there you have it; a few interesting facts about the cakes we take so much for granted. Like everything else evolving with time, cakes have their moments in history too. Next time you enjoy your cake, think of all the human inventions needed over time, necessary to allow you this little luxury.

INGREDIENTS USED IN CAKE PREPARATION

The ingredients used to make shortened (butter) and un –shortened (foam) cakes differ. However, the goal is always to the same: to create great cake recipes through a delicate balance of its ingredients – making sure they have the strength to hold the recipe together, but still create a tender, moist and flavorful cake. Most cakes are created from liquid batters with high fat and sugar contents. The baker's job is to combine all the ingredients to create a structure that will support these rich ingredients yet keep the cake as light and delicate as possible. As with other baked goods, it is impossible to taste a cake until it is fully cooked and too late to alter the formula. Therefore, it is extremely important to study any formula before beginning and to follow it with particular care and attention to detail.

<u>Cake making ingredients are classified as:</u>

- Essential ingredients: Flour, sugar, shortening, milk and eggs.
- Optional ingredients: Baking powder, flavourings and essences, fruits, nuts, cocoa powder, chocolate, cake improvers, syrups etc.

<u>Ingredients are also classified according to the function which they perform in cake making.</u>

- Structure builders: Flour, eggs, milk and shortenings.
- Tenderizers: fat, sugar, baking powder and egg yolks.
- Dryers: Flour, starches and dry milk powder
- Toughners: Flour, dry milk powder and egg whites.
- Favorers: Butter, eggs, vanilla or other flavorings, liquid and salt.
- Moisteners: milk or water, liquor, egg, syrups and sugar.

1. **Flour:** Vast majority of cakes – with the exception of cheesecakes, foam cakes and gluten –free cakes – contain wheat flour as very backbone of their composition. It establishes the crumb structure in cakes and is used to bind all of the other ingredients together during the cake making process. Wheat flour contains two very important proteins, *glutenin* and *gliadin*, when mixed with moisture and stirred, create its structural network. This protein content for cake making in flour should be 7 to 9 percent. Under low ph conditions,

starch gelatinizes faster and thus affects a faster setting of cake structure when baked. The bad part about gluten is that too much – from too much mixing or using the wrong type of flour – creates a tough, dry and flavorless cake. It's gluten from the wheat flour that gives dough its strength and elasticity – qualities we want in yeast breads, but not in cakes. Cakes made from strong flour will peak in the center and will be tough and dry to eat. In case of too weak flour, the cakes may flatten out or even sink.

To help prevent this, you'll see cake recipes especially high –ratio ones, typically made with chlorinated soft wheat flours, such as bleached cake flour, a potentially containing low –gluten forming proteins. (High ratio cakes are where the sugar is higher than the flour level, by weight.) Other lower gluten flour types include Southern bleached all –purpose and pastry flour. Soft wheat flours are generally low in water absorption and do not require harsh mixing or a long mix time.

Chlorination of cake flour provides two great benefits. First is bleaching, which gives a bright whiter crumb color to cakes but second and more importantly it lowers the gelatinization temperature of the starch within the cake flour. This makes it possible for the cake to set faster and therefore reduces the loss of leavening during baking. Bleaching also gives the cake flour the ability to carry more sugar and fat (as well as water), without their tenderizing (collapsing) effects, balancing the recipe.

1. **Sweeteners –Caster sugar, Icing sugar, Brown sugars:** We typically think of sugar's role in a cake recipe to add sweetness, but it also plays other important roles

depending upon whether it is in the crystalline (granulated white, caster or brown) or liquid form (honey or corn syrup). All sugar acts as a tenderizer by preventing the wheat flour proteins from forming an excessive amount of gluten and slows down the coagulation of the egg white and milk proteins, as well, it also contribute to structure of the cake when baked. It does this because sugar is hygroscopic, another word for its ability to absorb or attract moisture from the air, and dissolve readily in it (honey and some liquid sugars are more hygroscopic than crystalline sugar). By doing so, sugar essentially absorbs available water in the recipe, until saturated, leaving the rest for the wheat's available gluten forming proteins. Gluten is formed when the wheat flour protein's are moistened and agitated or mixed; the higher the flour's gluten –forming potential, the more available water or liquid and the more mixing (agitation) that takes place and the less tenderizers, such as sugar and fat, (and the warmer the ingredients), the more gluten is formed. Also because of its hygroscopic nature, it helps with a recipe's moisture retention and thus increases its shelf life by slowing the staling process.

Most commonly used crystalline sugar or sucrose plays an important role by incorporating air into the batter for leavening when beaten with butter or margarine or solid shortening, called "creaming" (only when the fat is at an optimal temperature). Sugar plays an important role with the lubrication of other ingredients in the recipe, when *caramelized*, golden brown coloured crust is formed. Increasing sugar in a cake recipe will raise the gelatinization temperature of the starches in the wheat flour and thus will increase expansion time, so care must be taken in its ratio to the other ingredients; too much can cause a cake's structure to fail or the cake may be so tenderized that it crumbles when cut rather than staying in slices (a warm cake will also cause crumbling). When the sugar is reduced too much, the gluten structure is so strong that the cake develops some long cells or tunnels. Overall volume may even increase, but the cake would be tough.

Other types of sugars used in the cakes include dextrose, caster, icing and brown sugar. Also syrups such as invert sugar, corn syrup, glucose, molasses, honey, sorbitol or refiner's syrups are used in part with powdered sugar for their special characteristics. When using these sweetener varieties you must be aware that some do not have the same sweetness as granulated sugar (sucrose) and do contain various levels of water. Sugars of any kind when used in cakes tend to soften the batter and make it thinner, and they need to be included as liquids. Coarse grained sugar, also known as superfine sugar is used to help create the finest texture and maximum volume in a cake. Too large grain will have cutting action on fat which will prevent entrapping of air cells during creaming operation. Too fine grain will also not produce desirable aeration. Sugar can stand in for fat and is often added to commercial low –fat products or recipes.

3. **Fats and shortenings:** There are four types of fat and shortening available; Butter, lard, hydrogenated fat and margarine. The primary function of solid fat, also known as plastic fat, solid shortening, stick butter or margarine, is to incorporate innumerable air bubbles into its malleable mass for volume. This is done through creaming, or beating the fat with crystalline sugar, also

known as white granulated or brown sugar (white granulated sugar combined with molasses). But, it can only be done successfully if the right ingredients, ratios, mixing times and temperature (70^0F -75^0F), and using the proper tools are followed. Too hard fat will not cream up well wile too soft fats will not be able to retain the aeration. Fats have a tenderizing action on the flour proteins and thus expanding the air cells and helping to lift the cake's batter during baking, resulting in eventual cake tenderness. They are also known as shorteners; they also shorten the length of the gluten strands when the flour is stirred with that moisture. Fats also tenderize by readily coating the flour proteins like a raincoat, during mixing, preventing moisture from reaching them, helping to reduce their gluten forming potential and improving the shelf life. Fat is also a good tenderizer because it slows down the coagulation of the egg with the flour and milk proteins that set the structure of the cake when baked. Fat

Some fats, such as butter or hydrogenated fatimpart taste and flavor to a cake, whereas margarine does not have as fine a texture and taste. Shortening does not contribute flavor, unless you use the "butter flavored" type.

4. **Eggs:** Eggs perform a multitude of important functions in a cake recipe, depending on the part used. Foamed eggs provide leavening, especially separated and beaten whites. Whole eggs and whites contribute to structure of the cakes. Egg yolk is also a rich source of emulsifying agents Lecithin and, thus, is a tenderizer thus facilitating the incorporation of air during creaming or whipping process and inhibits wheat starch gelatinization. Egg

yolks also add color (due to the presence of Luthein), nutrition, and flavor and help to retain moisture in the finished cake. Eggs also act as binding agents and thus improve sustainability. On the other hand, whites can have a drying effect, but they contribute slightly more protein than yolks do, although with far fewer nutrients and without the fat and cholesterol.

5. **Leaveners:** A leaven, often called a leavening agent (and also known as a raising agent), is any one of a number of substances used in doughs and batters that cause a foaming action (gas bubbles) that lightens and softens. It starts with the creation of millions of tiny air bubbles from various mixing methods, trapped in the structural framework of the cake's batter by the gluten strands. Air incorporation comes from beating eggs, creaming butter and sugar together, from folding ingredients together, and from any agitation. Cakes are then leavened when the air bubbles in their batters expand when heated from water vapor or steam from liquids. The type of leavener to be used is based upon the kind of cake required for, according to volume, taste, flavour, colour, structure and consistency. Leaveners can be of three kinds – chemical leaveners, biological leaveners and mechanical aeration.

CHEMICAL LEAVENERS–

Baking Powder –made from Cream of tartarand sodium bicarbonate and starch, is a leavening agent, which causes your batter to rise. It is available in two forms: single acting baking powder – which acts instantly and the cakes has to be baked immediately as soon as it is mixed. Double acting powders – In this some of the gas is released when it is mixed to the batter at room temperature and the final gas is released in the oven when it faces high temperature. Too much baking powder results in a bitter tasting product, while too little results in a tough cake with little volume.

Baking Soda –Baking soda is pure *sodium bicarbonate,* and needs to be paired with an acidic ingredient like honey, chocolate, or yogurt so that carbon dioxide is released due to reaction. This carbon dioxide expands in volume in the oven causing the product to rise. It is used in the production of rich red colour speciality cakes, but use of too much will result in a soapy, coarse cake. Since it reacts immediately, so it is recommended for recipes which call for soda immediately or else the product will fall flat.

A chemical leavening agent provides a source of gas to the recipe called carbon dioxide. When moistened (baking soda and double acting baking powder) and/or heated (double acting baking powder), it expands the millions of air bubbles previously created in a batter or dough from mixing or any agitation made to the cake's ingredients, trapped in the structural framework by the gluten strands. If the batter is over mixed, becomes too warm or not baked promptly, the gas will escape and the final recipe will have poor texture and low volume. One of the biggest failures of a cake recipe is using baking powder or baking soda that has been weakened from being moistened previously in the cabinet or refrigerator from humidity. Another failure can be caused by pre –wetting a chemical leavened batter because they start to release carbon dioxide bubbles immediately (double acting baking powder will again leaven when heated). Refrigeration will slow their release, but not stop it. Also, when a batter is placed in an oven that has not been preheated, baking powder fails to act until the oven reaches over 120 degrees F. Using the wrong flour can also affect leavening.

BIOLOGICAL LEAVENERS These include Saccharomyces cerevisiae producing carbon dioxide found in: baker's yeast, beer (unpasteurised—live yeast) ginger beer, and Kefir and sourdough starter. Clostridium perfringens producing hydrogen found in salt – rising bread. Compressed yeast is also called cake yeast, because of its use in cake making. Yeast cakes have texturethat is closer to a Brioche or a sweet roll instead of a sponge cake. Some also call for trimming off the browned crust and just using the soft interior. Yeast raised dough is supported by the protein structure of gluten while cakes made with baking powder and baking soda are supported by a starch structure. Recipes like yeast cakes, coffee cakes etc. using yeast usually also call for bread (strong) flour which has a higher protein content (12%) than all purpose (regular) flour (8%). Cake recipes using baking soda or baking powder usually call for cake flour which has less protein (3%) than that of normal flour.

MECHANICAL AERATION – while creaming fat and sugar or fat and flour or beating egg with or without sugar. When ingredients are beaten or whisked together using hand, spatula, whisk or the appropriate attachments on a machine/blender and no baking powder used it is considered to be mechanically aerated. Sponge goods are good example as the egg and sugar are whisked to a peak and then the flour is folded in, no other form of aeration is used.The surface area will strive to remain at a minimum thus offering a resistance which drives the mixture behind the beating equipment as it penetrates still further into the mix. It is during this fractional moment of time before the beater strikes again that air bubbles are drawn into the mixing until at last it is thoroughly aerated. Cake contains moisture and when it is heated, the moisture turns into steam which causes into raised volume of the product.

6. **Dairy and Liquids:** Milk is usually the main liquid dairy used in cake recipes. It hydrates the dry ingredients, dissolves the sugar and salt, provides steam for leavening and allows for the baking powder and/or baking soda to react and produce carbon dioxide gas. Milk contains proteins (caseins) that set or coagulate from the oven's heat and help form the structure of the cake, as do flour and eggs. It enriches the cake nutritionally and improves flavor and taste of cakes. Lactose sugar present in milk improves the crust colour and moisture retention capacity of cakes. Water vapour also leavens the cakes thereby acting as a tenderizer.

    Other dairy products, such as buttermilk, sour cream or cream cheese add more moisture and flavor to a cake; consequently those made with them keep well. The acid in the buttermilk and sour cream help tenderize the gluten in the recipe, producing a finer crumb. Sour cream and cream cheese add richness to a recipe, which makes them moist and almost springy.Shelf life of cakes is determined by the amount of moisture retained in the cake which eventually depends upon the amount of water used. Other liquids than are used or can be used include rum, wine, fruit juices, sherbets etc.

7. **Flavorings and Essences:** These are the ingredients that add distinction and character to baked goods. Flavour can come from wet ingredients or dry ingredients, for

example, we use a sprinkle of cocoa powder to give an added depth of chocolate. Flavorings and essences come in different forms: ground spices, extracts (especially pure vanilla extract), citrus zest (peel), citrus oil and even liqueurs. Essence in general term that can mean an oil, extract or concentrated substance made from an animal or vegetable. Oils are generally available in the pure form, containing no alcohol or water. It must be used sparingly. Extracts are diluted oils; usually containing about 20% pure oil and the rest are additives. Alcohol is frequently used as an additive. Flavourings and essences can broadly be divided into artificial (or synthetic) flavourings and natural flavourings e.g. pure vanilla essence, orange, pineapple, strawberry etc. the role of an essence is to impart flavour and it is always added to the batter just before baking, so as to retain the flavour in the batter.

Flower Essences: Baking with flower essences can add a subtle, perfumed flavour to cake sponges, cookies and frostings. Violet, lavender and rose essences are some of the most popular flower essence flavours.

Fruit Essences: Using a fruit essence rather than fruit itself can give a more intense flavour. It also means fruit doesn't have to be added to the sponge which can alter both the texture and colour. Strawberry, raspberry, and blueberry are all delicious berry essences, while orange and lemon bring a sharper citrus flavour. Banana essence gives a powerful synthetic banana flavour, so add little by little so as not to overdo it.

Candy Essences: Candy oils come in a wide range of flavors, such as orange, lime or lemon flavors, tangerine, cherry, etc.

Nut Essences: For a delicious nutty flavour, a splash or two of nut essence can transform your cakes and cookies. Almond and hazelnut work especially well when paired with other ingredients in your cake such as fruit and chocolate. If you have a nut allergy, avoid nut essences as you would any nut ingredients.

Bean essences: Vanilla bean paste is a much thicker mixture of vanilla beans, sugar and water and can be used sparingly as an alternative to vanilla extract.

Other essences commonly used in baking include coffee, rum, brandy and coconut.

8. **Salt:** Salt or sodium chloride is an important ingredient in cake making. It is generally added at the later state while baking cakes. Without salt the cake will taste flat. Usually only a pinch of salt is added, but the amount of salt added may differ according to the amount of flour/ salted butter used. It should be such that the salty flavor should not be discernible. Depending upon the method of combining ingredients, salt can also have a strengthening effect if it's combined with egg whites. If whipped egg whites to which salt has been added are "folded in," they're better able to hold their volume. Although salt is not considered to be an aid in leavening, it can contribute slightly to the volume of some recipes. It gives a balance to the sweetness and other flavors during baking, moistens the cake (as it is hygroscopic in nature) and also improves the crust colour of cakes by lowering the caramelization temperature of sugar.

9. **Emulsifiers:** Convenience, fast aeration, uniform performance, stable production, and stability in the end product are all key factors when considering the perfect cake emulsifier for industrial cake production.

Oil and water are immiscible since the interaction results in high energy at the common surface. Through the physical action of mixing one can break up the oil into fine droplets which may be dispersed/ distributed into the water phase to form a dispersion which may be called an emulsion. An emulsion is an unstable multiphase system containing at least two immiscible liquid phases. When the physical mixing action is stopped the oil droplets will coalesce and the oil and water will again separate into 2 different layers. To stabilize an emulsion, the droplets of the disperse phase must be as small as possible and as widely distributed as possible in the continuous phase. Further the viscosity of the continuous phase must be high to retard coalescence. Ultimately to prevent such coalescing of oil droplets and subsequent layer separation, certain chemicals may be used which are known as emulsifiers. In other words emulsions act as a hook between water phase and oil phase and prevent them from separating. This activity keeps the water evenly distributed in the cake batter with considerably reduced rate of evaporation and thus increasing shelf life. It also helps the fat to get distributed evenly in the batter, thus the air cells are also evenly distributed which leaven the cake and give good volume.

Emulsifiers are made up of molecules that have a non –polar (fatty acid) end which carries no charge and has an affinity for oil and a polar (glycerol) end which carries a charge and has an affinity for water. Such a molecule can situate itself at the interface between oil and water. The polar end will immerse itself in the aqueous phase and the non –polar end will immerse itself in the lipid phase and prevent coalescence of the oil droplets. This helps the two phases to stay intimately mixed and form a stable emulsion.

As cake baking has become a more precise industrial activity, baking emulsifiers have become a very important class of ingredients in the manufacture of cakes and other sweet goods. Good example of emulsifiers are: DATEM (emulsifier E 472e), Lecithin, SSL and CSL (sodium and calcium stearoyl lactylates).

10. **Dry Fruits and Nuts:** These are of specific organoleptic characteristics (flavour, taste and consistency) and are used depending upon the choice. Traditionally dried fruits and nuts are used as they generally do not add moisture to the cakes. Commonly used fruits and nuts are raisins, currants, sultanas, hazel nuts, walnuts, figs, mixed peel and glace cherries.

11. **Spices:** Spice is easily one of the best cake flavors around. Common spices used in baking include ground cinnamon, ground mixed spice, ground ginger and nutmeg. It's worth having jars of these to hand and buying others as needed. Few marked specialty spiced cakes may be: buttermilk spice cake, spice Bundt cake, carrot cake, gingerbread spice cake, pumpkin cake etc.

12. **Chocolate:** It's worth having some plain chocolate in your store cupboard for making chocolate cakes; for breaking up to use as chocolate chips and for making rich chocolate cake toppings. In most recipes a plain chocolate of around 40 per cent cocoa solids is adequate unless otherwise stated. Chocolates provide colour, texture, moisture, flavour and taste to cakes.

13. **Cocoa:** Another key ingredient for chocolate cake recipes, cocoa provides an intense chocolate flavour. It

has the benefit of not needing to be melted and is completely stable. A couple of tbsps are often used in place of flour in addition to melted chocolate to give depth to the recipe. It is also used when making chocolate butter cream for icing and filling cakes.

There are other ingredients that frequently feature in recipes which you might also like to have at the ready if you bake regularly. These include:

- **Black treacle** – This is often used in rich fruit cakes and other full –flavoured bakes.
- **Candied peel** – Made from sugared citrus fruits, candied peel is frequently used in Christmas cakes, panettone and Florentine biscuits.
- **Desiccated coconut** – If you like coconut –flavoured cakes or cakes spread with jam and dipped in coconut then keep a packet of unsweetened desiccated coconut to hand.
- **Dried fruit** – If you're a fruit cake fan, it's good to have a bag of currants, sultanas and raisins in the cupboard. There are plenty of other dried fruits available so buy them as you need them or select your favorites to modify a recipe.
- **Glacé cherries** –You can buy either the bright red glacé cherries which are dyed or the deeper red un –dyed cherries for use in fruit cakes, particularly Christmas cake.
- **Golden syrup** – Sticky and sweet, golden syrup makes a moist sticky cake and, like black treacle, keeps for a long time in the cupboard.
- **Ground almonds** – Ground almonds are often used in place of flour or as well as flour in cake recipes. They

produce a moist cake and are suitable as a gluten –free option.

- **Honey** – Honey is often used in addition to sugar and creates a moist and fragrant cake.
- **Jam** –Smooth apricot jam is a must if you like to make celebration cakes as it's used to stick marzipan on to fruit cake. Strawberry or raspberry jams are also good as a filling for a Victoria sandwich.
- **Lemons, limes, oranges** – A little bit of zest can liven up a plain sponge mix. Some recipes also require the juice to make a sugar syrup for drizzling.
- **Nuts** – Mixed chopped nuts, walnut halves, hazelnuts, flaked almonds and pecans are among the nuts you might want to have on hand. Again, choose the ones you like the best. Often one type of nut can be substituted for another in recipes. Store nuts in airtight containers as they might get rancid in contact to air.
- **Polenta** – Polenta is another flour substitute – cakes made with this ingredient tend to be denser, pleasantly textured and have a vibrant yellow colour.
- **Sunflower oil** – Sunflower oil has many culinary uses and it's ideal for baking as it has a mild flavour which allows the other ingredients in a cake to shine through.
- **Food Colours** – This is an important constituent of cake as every cake is associated with a certain type of colour. Addition of colour it gives the food an attractive and appetizing appearance. Dyes of various colours (most commonly blue, green, red and yellow) are used to the cakes. Food colorings are available in small to big bottles in liquid form and in wide variety of colors.

CHAPTER FIFTEEN

CLASSIFICATION OF CAKES

There are many different types of cakes and many different ways of dividing them into various categories, but professional bakers categorize cakes by ingredients and mixing method. (Home bakers tend to categorize cakes by flavoring –i.e., chocolate cakes, fruit cakes, and so on –which is helpful when you're trying to decide what to eat, but not as helpful when you're trying to understand how best to make a cake.) Depending on how the batter is prepared, you will find that the final texture (and color, if it is a yellow or white cake) varies. Below is a comprehensive but by no means exhaustive list of the basic types of cakes:

SHORTENED (FAT OR OIL) CAKES

These contain some kind of fat—often butter, but sometimes oil—and baking powder to leaven them or make them rise. If the fat is butter, the ingredients are usually combined using the creaming method, which means that the soft butter and sugar are beaten together in an electric mixer to partially dissolve the sugar and to incorporate some air. Then the dry and wet ingredients are added in alternating doses. This results in a light and airy crumb, though not quite as light as that of a sponge cake. The best butter cakes have a moist buttery richness tempered by lightness. Included in this category are:

Pound cakes: This is the simplest type of butter cake. A classic pound cake is made with a pound each of butter, sugar, eggs, and flour. This produces a dense yet tender texture. Pound cakes are heavier than the types of butter cakes used for constructing layer cakes. They're easy to prepare, with the only trick being that the butter must be quite soft when you begin. These cakes are usually very lightly flavored and served plain or topped with a simple glaze or water icing. A pound cake is usually baked in a loaf or Bundt pan. Many coffee cakes, sour cream cakes, and fruit crumb cakes are variations of pound cake.

Butter (and oil) layer cakes: Many different types of cake can be arranged in layers. However, classic American layer cakes are usually butter or oil cakes. The birthday cake you ate as a child was probably of this type. These cakes are lighter than traditional pound cake, but more moist and flavorful than European –style sponge layer cakes. Cakes in this category include: devil's food cake (the classic chocolate layer cake), golden cakes (made with egg yolks, which add richness and a golden color), and white cakes (made with egg whites, which create a lighter, whiter colored cake).

SPONGE AND FOAM CAKES

These are notable more for what they are missing than for what they contain: They usually do not include fat, such as butter or oil, and they do not incorporate leaveners, like baking powder. Instead, volume is created by **whipping the eggs** or egg whites. The air whipped into the eggs expands during baking, causing these cakes to rise on their own without baking powder. However, the success of this method depends on not deflating the eggs after whipping them. To this end, dry ingredients are usually sifted over and gently folded in, and fat is often avoided, as it would weigh down the foamy batter.

This method produces extremely light, airy cakes with a spongy texture but generally less flavor and moisture than butter and oil cakes. The basic types of sponge and foam cakes are:

Angel Food Cake: This type is made with egg whites alone and no yolks. The whites are whipped with sugar until very firm before the flour is gently folded in, resulting in a snowy –white, airy, and delicate cake that marries beautifully with fruit. Most angel food cakes have a spongy, chewy quality derived from their relatively high sugar content and the absence of egg yolks. Baked in ungreased two –piece tube pans, angel food cakes are cooled by being inverted, since this type of cake would collapse if cooled right –side –up in the pan or if removed from the pan while still warm.

Genoese: This type of sponge cake is made with whole eggs rather than just egg whites, which gives it a richer flavor than angel food cake. The eggs are combined with sugar and gently heated over simmering water, then whipped (heating the eggs allows them to be whipped to a greater volume). Genoese lacks much assertive flavor of its own, but it is often used to construct layered or rolled cakes when a lighter texture than a butter cake is desired. To add flavor and moisture, Genoese cake layers are always moistened with flavored syrup, and they are often sliced into thin horizontal layers and stacked with rich fillings such as butter cream. These layer cakes, common in the coffeehouses of Europe, are called "European –style" to distinguish them from American –style butter layer cakes, which generally have fewer, thicker layers.

Biscuit (always pronounced the French way as *bees –kwee*): This type of sponge cake contains both egg whites and yolks, but, unlike in Genoese, the whites and yolks are whipped separately and then folded back together. This creates a light batter that's drier than a Genoese but holds its shape better after mixing. For this reason, it's often used for piped shapes such as ladyfingers. If baked in a tube pan like an angel food cake, it makes a very chewy sponge cake that was popular in the early 20th century but has since fallen out of favor. However, it's still known in a slightly different form as the classic Passover sponge cake, in which the flour is replaced by matzoh cake meal and potato starch.

Chiffon Cake: This fairly recent American creation was invented by a salesman who sold the recipe to General Mills, which spread the recipe through marketing materials in the 1940s and 1950s. A classic chiffon cake is kind of a cross between an oil cake and a sponge cake. It includes baking powder and vegetable oil, but the eggs are separated and the whites are beaten to soft peaks before being folded into the batter. This creates a cake with a tender crumb and rich flavor like an oil cake, but with a lighter texture that's more like a sponge cake. Chiffon cakes can be baked in tube pans like angel food cakes or layered with fillings and frostings.

LOW – OR NO –FLOUR CAKES

Cakes made without flour (or with very little) generally have a creamy or silky texture. They can be baked or unbaked

Baked Flourless:

These include baked cheesecakes and flourless chocolate. For easy removal, they're often made in a spring form pan, though some can also be made in regular round layer cake pans. Often the filled pan is placed in a larger pan that's half –filled with water to insulate the delicate, creamy cake from the oven's strong bottom h at, which might give the baked cake a porous rather than silky texture. This is called baking the cake in a water bath.

Unbaked Flourless Cakes:

These types of cakes are typically molded in a dessert ring or spring form pan then simply chilled before unmolding. They include unbaked cheesecakes and mousse cakes. They often have a crust or bottom layer that's baked before the mousse is added. Sometimes other layers, such as Genoese or biscuit, are alternated with the mousse.

CHAPTER SIXTEEN

CAKE MAKING METHODS

Cake making methods can be divided into two main categories:

Shortened cakes – In shortened category there are 4 methods of mixing

1. Creaming method or sugar batter method
2. Two stage method or blending method
3. Flour batter method
4. Sugar batter method

Egg foam method

1. Sponge method
2. Angel food method
3. Chiffon method

The 3 main goals of cake making are:

- To combine ingredients into a smooth uniform batter.
- To form and incorporate air cells in the batter.
- To develop a proper texture in the finished product.

SHORTENED CAKES – *In short end category there are 4 methods of mixing*

Creaming Method: This is the conventional method used for many cookie doughs, butter cakes, and pound cakes. It was for a long time the standard method for mixing high –fat (butter) cakes. Butter cakes are highly prized for their flavor; shortening adds no flavor to cakes. Butter also influences texture because it melts in the mouth, while shortening does not. However, many bakers may prefer to substitute shortening for all or part of the butter in these formulas. Shortening has the advantage of being less expensive and easier to mix. In creaming recipes, use regular shortening, not emulsified shortening. Regular shortening has better creaming abilities. Examples – cookies, marble cake, choco chips brownies, cup cake etc.

Method – The creaming method starts out with softened, solid fat (such as butter or margarine). All fats used should be at room temperature. Very hard shortenings will not cream up well while too soft shortenings will not be able to retain aeration. The fat is then mixed with granulated or brown or powdered sugar which is added gradually. Granular fats should be avoided which have poor whipping quality. The creaming comes into play as the fat is mashed against the sides with the sand –like sugar crystals working against it, softening it even more while forcing air into it. Creaming should be done at a low to medium speed. A high speed may melt the fat, causing a loss of air bubbles. Creaming for too long creates a coarse texture in the finished cake. When adequate aeration is achieved, the mixture becomes very light, fluffy and brighter in appearance. Eggs are added gradually. Eggs should be at room temperature. Before adding the eggs they should be whipped to the stiff consistency and small amount of flour is added to it so that the mixture doesn't curdle. If the batter is curdled, there is a loss of aeration which results in low volume and poor texture of cakes. The air cells of the whipped eggs either diffuse into the air cells already present or increase the number of air cells in the cream and the liquid part of the egg is evenly distributed in the mixture giving it a smooth , velvety appearance. Liquids such as liquid sugars, water, milk, fruit juices, fruit pulp, etc along with essences and colour can be added at this stge. This is done in order to have sufficient moisture in the mix to prevent toughening of gluten while mixing flour. Next stage is to incorporate flour in the mixture. Flour should be sifted with other ingredients such as baking powder or soda etc in order to ensure its thorough dispersal. It has to be mixed with minimum possible of mixing action.

Two Stage Method: This is a simple, foolproof way of mixing a cake base, using very few steps in the process. This method was developed for use with modern high ratio shortening. High ratio cakes contain a large percentage of sugar more than 100% based on the weight of the flour. Also they are made with more liquids than creaming method cakes. This method is often used to make cakes in high volumes bakeries. This method is typically used when a recipe contains a higher portion of sugar than flour by weight. Emulsified shortening, such as the high –ratio variety, is used because the amount of liquid ingredients is also proportionally larger than, for example, in the foaming or creaming methods. This type of batter is always leavened with a chemical agent (baking soda and/or baking powder) rather than relying solely on the air incorporated with a whip. Whole eggs, granulated sugar, cake flour, and baking powder are placed in a mixer and stirred at low speed to form a paste. Emulsified shortening is added and the mixture is whipped at high speed for two minutes. Milk or water is then added along with a flavoring, such as vanilla extract. The batter is whipped at high speed one minute longer. Example – Yellow cake

Method – Scale all the ingredients. Have all the ingredients at room temperature. Sift the flour, baking powder, soda, salt etc in the mixing bowl and add the shortening and mix. Sift the remaining dry ingredients into the bowl and add part of water or milk. Mix slowly. Scrape down the sides from time to time to ensure even mixing. Combine the remaining liquids and lightly beaten eggs and add this mixture to the batter in 3 parts. Continue to mix to form produce a smooth and homogenous batter. The finished batter is normally quite liquid. The mixture is now ready for panning and baking.

Flour Batter Method: The following procedure is used only for a few specialty items. It produces a fine –textured cake, but there may be some toughening due to the development of gluten. Flour –batter cakes include those made with either emulsified shortening or butter or both. Fat and an equal weight of flour are creamed together till it becomes light and fluffy.

Method – In the flout batter method, the flour is added as two separate portions firstly mixed with the creamed ingredients with a second portion added later to the batter. The flour and fat are mixed together, while the eggs and sugar are whisked together in a separate bowl. The fat is usually creamed with a similar amount of flour, for example: 400g flour to 450g fat to obtain a suitable creamy mixture until the flour particles are thoroughly coated with fat. Once the eggs and sugar are sufficiently whisked to form foam they are added in small portions to the flour and fat mix. Once these two portions are combined together in a cohesive batter any additional flour is added. The mixed batter should be deposited into cake pans and baked without delay. It must be kept in mind that once the leavening agents have been added to the batter, they begin to react and evolve carbon dioxide gas

Sugar Batter Method: The sugar batter is based on the emulsion of oil in water with air bubbles being trapped in the fat phase while other ingredients are dissolved in the water phase.

Method – The fat and sugar are creamed depending on the temperature and creaming quality of the fat at medium speed to produce a fluffy and light in coloured mixture. During this stage, small air cells are formed which are entrapped into the creamed mixture. This mixture takes on volume and becomes lighter in consistency. The exact time for proper creaming at this stage is will depend on several factors like temperature of the fat and the speed of the mixing machine – High speed will create friction and tends to destroy the number of air cells that are formed and incorporated during the early stages of mixing. The liquid egg is added in 4 –5 portions with creaming in between each addition to prevent any curdling occurring and producing a batter that is smooth and has a velvety appearance and texture. In the final stages of the creaming method of mixing sifted flour and any additional water, milk or essence is then gently added to the batter.

EGG FOAM METHOD

The egg foam method is the method we use to make Genoese, French macaroons, sponge cake, and angel food cake, among others. Batters made using this method are generally very low in fat, often having no extra fat added, except the fat in the egg yolks, if whole eggs are called for. Egg –foam cakes have a springy texture and are tougher than shortened cakes. This makes them valuable for many kinds of desserts that require much handling to assemble. The egg foam method relies on the leavening power of eggs and steam to create the lift necessary to make a delicate angel food cake or Genoese. The method mostly starts by whipping of eggs (egg whites for Sponge cakes and whole eggs for Genoese) and sugar until they turn light. Sift dry ingredients i.e. flour over the egg mixture and gently but thoroughly fold together all the ingredients. Don't dump the flour or you will break a lot of your bubbles and have a flat cake.

Method – The method mostly starts by whipping of eggs and sugar until they turn light. Sift dry ingredients i.e. flour over the egg mixture and gently but thoroughly fold together all the ingredients. Don't dump the flour or you will break a lot of your bubbles and have a flat cake. Foam cake methods use beaten eggs to give the cake volume.

Sponge Method: Sponge cakes are made from the three ingredients no baker can do without––eggs, sugar, and flour––although some sponges also contain butter. Classically made sponge cakes (Genoese in French) do not contain baking powder or baking soda; their volume and light texture come solely from the air whipped into the eggs. Sponge contains equal parts eggs, sugar, and flour. The weight of the eggs is always used as the basis for determining the quantity of the remaining ingredients. Whole eggs, entirely or in part, may be replaced with egg yolks or egg whites. More egg yolks will result in a denser sponge with finer pores. Increasing the amount of egg whites produces a lighter sponge with a larger pore structure. Increasing the yolk content in an already heavy sponge cake can have a detrimental effect. Granulated sugar or, even better, the finer grade castor sugar, should always be used in a sponge cake to ensure that the sugar dissolves easily. The flour used in a sponge cake must have a good ratio between starch and protein. Some gluten (a high percentage of which is found in bread flour, for instance), is necessary to bind and hold the structure, but too high a percentage makes the batter rubbery and hard to work with and results in a tough and chewy sponge. A flour with too much starch, such as cake flour, will produce a light and tender sponge, but the structure will collapse partially when baked. Flour for sponge cakes should always be sifted. If you use unsweetened cocoa powder or any other dry ingredient, sift it in with the flour. When adding the flour to the batter, not to break the air bubbles that you just whipped in. Fold in the flour with a rubber spatula or your hand and turn the mixing bowl slowly with your other hand at the same time to combine the ingredients evenly. Never stir the flour into the batter or add it with the mixer.

Butter can be added to a sponge in an amount up to two –thirds the weight of the sugar. The butter should be melted but not hot. It is always added last, after the flour has been completely incorporated. Chopped nuts or chopped candied fruit may be added to a sponge cake without changing the formula; provided it is a fairly heavy sponge (the pieces will settle on the bottom in a very light sponge batter).

Method – Scale all the ingredients accurately. Combine the eggs and sugar in a clean bowl. Immediately set the bowl over hot water until the mixture warms up to 43°C (for greater volume). If any liquid is included add it now at this stage only. Fold in sifted flour be careful not to deflate the volume. Immediately pan and bake the batter. Delay will cause loss of volume. Genoese is a variation of fatless sponge. Sponge method is of six types:

i. **Cold –Foaming Method** – In the cold –foaming method, the eggs and sugar are placed directly in the mixer bowl and whipped at high speed until creamy and light in color and the foam has reached its maximum volume. The butter can be added as well, but is generally left out since this method is typically used when the sponge will be soaked with a liqueur or flavoring, as in tiramisu or trifle, for example. Because part of the sugar melts in the oven rather than over the water bath as in the warm method, there are larger air bubbles in the finished sponge.

ii. **Warm –Foaming Method** – In the warm method, eggs and sugar are placed in a mixer bowl and stirred over immersing water (so that the eggs do not cook) to about 110°F (43°C) or until the sugar has dissolved completely. The mixture is removed from the heat and whipped at high speed until creamy and light in color and the foam has reached its maximum volume. Sifted flour is folded in, followed by the melted butter, if used. The main objective in the foaming method is to create a batter with the maximum amount of air.

iii. **Egg –Foaming Metho**d –In this method, the eggs are first separated; the yolks are whipped with part of the sugar to a light and fluffy consistency, and the whites and the remaining sugar are whipped to soft peaks. The yolks are gradually folded into the whites, followed by the sifted flour, part of which is replaced with finely ground nuts or almond paste, followed by any other ingredients, and, last, the melted butter, if used. Because this method produces a somewhat lighter sponge than the other two foaming methods, the sponge tends to shrink away from the sides of the pan more than is desirable. For this reason, it is best not to grease the sides of the cake pan. Instead, cut the baked sponge free using a sharp, thin knife.

iv. **Emulsifier – Method Sponge** –Another method and probably the most common in the baking industry today, is the emulsifier method; it is quick, convenient, and almost foolproof. The emulsifier is basically a whipping agent that contains a molecule that preserves the emulsion of lipids (fat) and water. By keeping the ingredients suspended and preventing separation, emulsifiers allow the batter to hold the air that has been whipped in without falling. In the emulsifier –method sponge, all ingredients, including the flour, are whipped together with the emulsifier for a specified time. The emulsifier method uses baking powder and does not rely on air as a leavening agent, so the sponge does not need to be baked immediately and can wait for its turn for the oven,

v. **Ladyfinger Sponge** – Another sponge variation is the ladyfinger sponge, also known as a piped sponge, which is used not only for cookies but also for several classic desserts, including tiramisu, charlotte Russe, and gateau Malakoff. In this method, more air is whipped into the batter so that it can be piped in to various shapes without running. Ladyfinger sponges are meant to be very dry after baking, but they easily absorb moisture from fillings or syrup.

vi. **Othello Sponge** –Othello sponge is comparable to the ladyfinger sponge, and the two are easily interchangeable. The Othello sponge has a lighter structure due to less flour and more egg white. The batter should immediately be piped out and baked as soon as it is finished, as the mixture becomes tough if left to stand too long.

Angel Food Method: This type of cake contains neither fat nor chemical leaveners. It relies solely on stabilized egg white foam for leavening. The foaming power of the egg whites results from a combined effort of various proteins to increase the thickness (viscosity) of the albumen and produce a fine mesh of foam (tiny bubbles) that will hold together for a time if properly combined with the sugar. Angel food batters have much higher sugar content than any other sponge or butter cake. Although sugar has a mixed influence in the whipping stage, where it acts to delay the foaming of the whites, it stabilizes the foam once it is whipped, especially in the oven, where sugar is necessary to prevent a total collapse. Sugar does this by forming hydrogen bonds and delaying evaporation. Mixing and baking an angel food cake successfully is a delicate procedure. Scale all the ingredients accurately. The egg whites may be slightly warmed in order to achieve better volume. Sift the flour with half the sugar. This helps the flour to mix more evenly with the egg whites. Beat the egg whites along with salt and cream of tartar until soft peak. Gradually add the sugar that was not mixed with flour. Beat until the egg whites form soft peaks. Do not beat until stiff. Fold in flour sugar mixture lightly and then bake it.

Method – Scale all the ingredients accurately. Te egg whites may be slightly warmed in order to achieve better volume. Sift the flour with half the sugar. This helps the flour to mix more evenly with the egg whites. Beat the egg whites along with salt and cream of tartar. Gradually add the sugar that was not mixed with flour. Beat until the egg whites form soft peaks. Do not beat until stiff. Fold in flour sugar mixture lightly and then bake it.

Chiffon Method: A chiffon cake is a very light cake made with vegetable oil, eggs, sugar, flour, baking powder, and flavorings. It is a combination of both butter and foam type (sponge type) cakes. Instead of the traditional cake ingredient butter or paste (such as shortening), vegetable oil is used; Chiffon cakes and angel food cakes are both based on egg –white foams, but here the similarities in the mixing methods end. In angel food cakes, a dry flour –sugar mixture is folded into the egg whites. In chiffon cakes, a batter containing flour, egg yolks, vegetable oil, and water is folded into the whites. Egg whites for chiffon cakes should be whipped until they are a little firmer than those for angel food cakes, but do not whip them until they are dry. Chiffon cakes contain baking powder, so they do not depend on the egg foam for all their leavening. A chiffon cake is a cross between an oil cake and a sponge cake. It includes baking powder and vegetable oil, but the eggs are separated and the whites are beaten before being folded into the batter creating the rich flavor like an oil cake, but with a lighter texture that's more like a sponge cake. They can be baked in tube pans or layered with fillings and frostings. The lack of butter, however, means that chiffon cakes lack much of the rich flavor of butter cakes.

Method – Scale all the ingredients. Use good quality flavorless vegetable oil. Sift the dry ingredients including part of sugar into a mixing bowl. Mixing with the paddle attachment gradually add oil, yolks, water and flavoring in a slow steady stream. Mix until smooth. Whip the egg whites along with cream of tartar, sugar to firm moist peaks. Fold the whipped egg whites in the flour liquid mixture. Deposit in pans and bake.

CHAPTER SEVENTEEN

CAKE IMPROVERS

Cake Improvers are "miracle ingredient." When added to cake batter at the creaming stage, it supposedly renders the crumb soft and moist and increases shelf life. The mysterious product contains rice starch, polyglycerol esters, and mono – and di –glycerides – the same additives found in many boxed cake mixes and commercial baked goods.

How Cake Improvers works: The addition of small amounts of certain forms of starch to cake batter mixes surprisingly and unexpectedly improve the basic important properties of the batter mix as shown both by the prebaked batter mix specific gravity as well as the substantially increased cake volumes obtained in the finished baked cakes. Moreover, it is found that in using these particular forms of starch, the finished baked cakes have extremely good crumb softness initially and can retain crumb softness over a storage period of six days. This fact is extremely important since the average family will not consume a cake on the same day that it is baked. Thus, the capability of a cake to retain a desirable level of softness for a long time is of prime concern. It is found that the addition of small quantities of a pre –gelatinized starch which does not contain more than about 18% by weight of amylase leads to vastly superior cake batter mixes and to the finished baked cakes obtained there from. While any form of pre –gelatinized low amylase – containing starch can be used. It effects in the batter mix system, such as hydration speed, quantity of absorbed water, extent of decreasing the specific gravity or the extent of increase in cake volume or the capacity to retain crumb softness in the finished baked cake is greatly improved. The starch must be pre –gelatinized before addition to a cake batter mix. Pre –gelatinization is carried out in conventional manner by heating the starch in the presence of excess water until the starch granules have broken and then the starch is dried upon drum rollers or any other form of conventional drying apparatus.

Various low amylase –containing starches may be incorporated in cake batter mixes, like waxy maize starches, waxy sorghum starches, starch ethers and esters, which are considered to contain at most trace amounts of amylase. An improved method of cake baking which comprises preparing a cake batter of principally flour, sugar and shortening and adding thereto from about 1% to about 5% of a pre –gelatinized starch which contains not more than 18% by weight of amylase, and then baking the said batter at elevated temperature to obtain an improved cake, said proportion of added pre –gelatinized starch being based upon the weight of solid ingredients in said batter.

In general the batter mix is capable of rapidly taking up water at high absorption levels so that the viscosity of the batter mix can be adequately increased. With a high viscosity the cake batter can entrap sufficient air during the mixing cycle with liquid components to provide a low specific gravity. A low specific gravity, in turn, will almost always yield finished baked cakes of adequate volume and good softness, texture and tenderness. Basically then, the desired properties in the batter mix system are rapid and high levels of hydration, high viscosity, and low specific gravity after the mixing cycle.

Cake gel is a cake improver, comprised of emulsifiers and humectants, which greatly improves volume through increased aeration and provides a more uniform crumb structure. It also improves softness in cake. Additionally, it increases batter stability and reduces variances that may be caused due to changing flour quantity and changing process parameters. Adding Cake gel helps in smooth mixing of all ingredients, improves batter consistency and strength, better and uniform crumb texture, extra volume and better eating qualities. It contains ingredients such as Emulsifiers, propylene glycol and water. It is to be added in the cake batter at a dosage of 3 to 8% on flour weight. (30g to 80g per 1kg flour).

What is a cake enhancer? : These fatty acids come from vegetable fats, and act as emulsifiers, allowing fats and liquids to combine more easily. They also serve as stabilizers and texture enhancers. Widely used in commercial baked products, they keep baked goods fresh and soft, and help cakes stay moist, light and fluffy and stay fresher longer.

CHAPTER EIGHTEEN

CAKE PRODUCTION

Cake batters are prepared using carefully tested formulas. Since these formulas are balanced, no changes should be made in the few ingredients that are added. For example, if the directions call for water to be added, do not add milk instead. Substituting ingredients or adding other ingredients will make the formula out of balance and can ruin the finished product. Follow the directions for a cake batter to get a good product. Cake baking is not difficult, but it requires some organization and forethought. While the steps for making a cake vary considerably depending on the type, you'll want to do the following before attempting any recipe:

1. **Read through the Recipe:** This sounds obvious, but cakes in particular have certain requirements, such as the temperature of ingredients, that cannot be altered. You don't want to realize too late that the butter you just mixed with sugar was supposed to be softened.

2. **Assemble ingredients and ensure Their Correct Temperature:** Get all of your ingredients and equipment out on the counter before you begin and

make sure they're at the proper temperature. This is especially important for butter and eggs: Soft butter makes for a smooth batter and a lofty cake, and room –temperature eggs keep the batter's temperature consistent.

To soften butter, leave it out for several hours; it should offer no resistance when you press on it. Or, you can hurry the process using a microwave: Cut the butter into ½–inch cubes, arrange them in a single layer on a microwave –safe plate, then microwave on high for 3 seconds at a time, testing in between, until the butter is softened but not melted.

3. **Preheat the Oven:** Before preparing the batter, your oven should be at the correct temperature. A batter will not react properly to heat if it sits at room temperature for 10 minutes waiting for the oven to heat. Nor will it rise properly if the oven continues to warm up after the pan has been placed in it. Avoid burning your cake by setting a rack in the middle of the oven for cake layers or in the lower third for a tube cake so that the top of the pan is not too close to the top of the oven.

4. **Prepare Your Equipment:** To ensure that your finished cake has the right shape, it's important to make sure that it will come out of the pan in one piece. The most common way to do this is to coat the pan with butter, but the specifics may vary depending on the type of cake. For cake layers in general, you coat the inside of the pan with very soft but not melted butter using a brush. Follow that with a disk of parchment paper cut to the size of the inside of the pan. For a butter cake baked

in a Bundt pan, coat with soft butter, and then coat the buttered surface with fine, dry bread crumbs, tapping the inverted pan to dislodge any excess. Follow with a quick coat of vegetable cooking spray for a guarantee that the cake won't stick. Line a rectangular or square pan with foil by molding the foil first on the back of the pan, then pressing it into the pan. Butter the foil. This makes it easy to lift a cake that you don't want to invert, such as a crumb cake, right out of the pan.

5. **Prepare the Batter:** Instructions will vary depending on the type of cake: For butter cakes, the ingredients will typically be combined using the creaming method; for sponge cakes the eggs will generally be beaten, then folded in. For the proper texture, be sure to follow the instructions closely, and then pour the batter into the pan or pans and bake.

6. **Test for Doneness:** To test a cake, plunge a thin knife or cake tester into the center (or halfway between the side and the tube if using a tube pan). When a cake is finished, you will find a few crumbs sticking to the knife or tester when you withdraw it. If the cake is not ready yet, there will be wet batter on the knife or tester.

7. **Cool the Cake:** Most cakes are cooled on a metal rack for even air circulation. A recipe will indicate whether the cake should be cooled in the pan or unmolded immediately. Follow instructions carefully—leaving certain types of cakes in the pan for too long may cause them to stick. Angel food cakes and chiffon cakes need to cool suspended upside down in their tube pans or they will deflate and look squashed and unappealing

when you cut them. Invert the pan over several inverted ramekins so that the edges of the pan are supported by them. It is best to figure out the system for doing this before you begin baking the cake by testing the empty pan over the ramekins to make sure your system will be stable.

8. **Unmold the Cake:** When you are ready, gently run a sharp, thin knife between the edge of the pan and the cake. Then invert a rack or platter (as indicated in the recipe) over the top of the pan. Turn the pan over and lift it off the cake. You may be asked to finish cooling the cake upside down or instructed to turn it right side up again. Be sure to follow instructions, as each type of cake cools best in a different way.

9. **"Finish" the cake:** As described in the section on fillings, frostings, and glazes, options for finishing a cake are numerous. Some varieties, such as pound cakes and crumb cakes, are finished already when they come out of the oven and don't need any embellishment at all. For others, a simple dusting of powdered sugar or quick brush with a glaze may be all that's required. And some cakes, such as European –style layer cakes, can be filled with multiple fillings, frosted with a different frosting or glaze, and then adorned with elaborate decorations, such as piped butter cream or marzipan crafted into roses and leaves.

It is to be noted that:

The oven temperature at which these cakes should be baked will vary over a considerable range, depending on factors such as richness of the formula, size of pan, and moisture content of the batter. Batters which are high in sugar content require low baking temperatures in the range of 325 – 350°F(160 –175°C), while leaner mixtures may be baked at a temperature range of 350 –400°F(175 – 200°C). The average baking time for layer cakes will take 15 –20 minutes and for cupcakes 10 –15 minutes.

Secrets to Baking Perfect Cakes:

Good results start in the mixing bowl: A cake is essentially a chemistry experiment—a series of ingredients mixed in a specific order to cause reactions that produce specific effects. Butter cakes, like pound cakes and most layer cakes, get their soft, fine texture and moistness—called a crumb—by first creaming together fat and sugar, adding eggs, and slowly incorporating dry ingredients into the mixture while alternating with a liquid, such as milk or buttermilk. Angel food, sponge, and chiffon cakes get their signature airy, foam like textures when whole eggs or egg whites (depending on the cake) are whipped until voluminous, and then folded into the batter. The air incorporated by whipping the eggs gives these cakes volume, making them springy and elastic. So whatever cake you're making, be sure to follow the recipe instruction closely. The order and method described really counts when cake baking.

Know your oven: To prevent an under – or overdone cake, get an oven thermometer—it's the best way to be sure your oven is calibrated correctly. Bake the cake in the middle (too close to the top or bottom can cause overbrowning). Gently close the oven door—a hard slam can release air bubbles trapped in the batter. To check for doneness, lightly press the center of the cake; if it springs back, it's done. Or insert a wooden pick; it should come out clean.

Choose the proper pan size (and color): Your recipe calls for two 9 –inch round cake pans, but you only have 8 –inch pans. What to do? Go get two 9 –inch pans. Pan size is specified in recipes because a cake increases in volume 50 to 100 percent during baking; if your pan is too small, the cake could overflow. Color is important, too; glass or dark nonstick pans usually require a 25 –degree reduction in baking temperature versus silver –colored aluminum pans.

Use the right flour for the recipe: Different flours contain varying percentages of protein—the more protein, the more gluten. Cake flour has the least protein and yields extra –light baked goods, like angel food cake. Bread flour has the most and is used for denser items; all –purpose is in the middle and produces tender cakes.

Weigh, don't measure, flour: If you don't have a kitchen scale, it's time to buy one. Weight is the only accurate way to measure flour. Depending on how tightly flour is packed into a measuring cup, you can end up with double the amount intended. That's why we give flour measurements in ounces first.

Chemistry counts: The intimate chemistry among key ingredients delivers the foundation for good cake. Flour thickens the batter and provides gluten, a protein that gives the cake structure. It forms when flour is combined with a liquid and agitated. Don't over mix, which can cause your cake to turn tough. Leaveners, like baking soda or powder, produce carbon dioxide bubbles, which are trapped by the starch in the batter and expand during baking, causing the cake to rise. Fats, like butter, shortening, or oil, help retard gluten formation while providing moisture for the cake. This ensures a tender texture. Sugar breaks up gluten, keeping the texture tender; it absorbs liquid, keeping the cake moist; and it caramelizes in baking, enriching flavors and helping the cake brown. Eggs firm up when cooked, helping cake batters set in the oven. Egg yolks contain fat, as well as lecithin, an emulsifier that allows fats and water to mix smoothly and ensures even texture.

Give your cake a cool down: Cool cakes in the pan on a wire rack for 20 minutes, and then remove from pan. Once cooled, place a plate on top, invert the pan, and gently tap or shake it to release the cake. Angel food cakes are usually baked in tube pans, then inverted either on feet attached to the pan or over a bottle to cool upside down while still in the pan—gravity helps the cake keep its volume. When it has cooled, run a narrow spatula around the edges, and release onto a plate.

Frost like a professional: Put a small dollop of frosting in the center of the cake plate, and place the first cake layer on top. This will keep the cake from moving as you work. Use an offset spatula to frost the top, add the next layer, then coat the whole cake with a thin layer of frosting.

(This "crumb coat" holds loose crumbs in place.) Place the cake in the freezer for 15 minutes, then remove and finish frosting, starting with the top, then the sides.

Fondant may make for a beautiful cake, but...: Rolled fondant—the smooth coating seen on elaborate wedding and reality –show competition cakes—is a combination of gelatin, glycerin, and sugar that forms into an easily molded dough. It doesn't taste very good, though. Poured fondant is cooked –sugar syrup that's used as a cake filling, in candies, or to top petit fours—you might know it better as the center of a Cadbury Crème Egg.

How to factor in a higher altitude: Since there is less air pressure at higher altitudes, cakes rise more and can dry out because liquids evaporate more quickly. If you live above 3,500 feet, follow these guidelines: Increase the oven temperature to 375° and liquid by 2 tbsps for each cup used. Decrease each cup of sugar by 1 tbsp, each tsp of baking powder by ⅛ tsp, and the baking time by 5 minutes.

CHAPTER NINETEEN

CAKE FORMULA BALANCING

What is a cake formula? It is an accurate record of the quantities of the raw materials necessary to make a particular type of cake. In other words.............. it is an accurate recipe.

If the recipe is correct, it will produce a good cake. As important as the recipe is the correct temperature, time and packing of the product. A good cake is one showing no faults, either in appearance, texture or while eating. It should be of good flavor and aroma and if it contains fruits, they must be evenly distributed. Bakery being the science that it is, we refer to the recipe as a *formula*. In the bakery, the range of ingredients that are used and which are essential is limited. There is Flour, Fat, Sweetening and Moistening. Each of these has a specific role to play and must be in *Balance* with each other.

What is balance? The ingredients that are used in cake making are divided according to their functions:

The tougheners – these are the ingredients that provide structure and form and give shape to the product. These will include flour and egg. The starch in the flour gelatinizes and the protein in the egg coagulates during baking and gives shape to the cake.

The softeners – these are the ingredients that soften the texture of the cake and include sugar and fat and milk. This softens the texture of cake and makes it different from that of bread, which contains basically the same ingredients but in a different proportion.

The moisteners – these ingredients like milk, egg and liquid sweeteners like golden syrup provide the moistening effect in the batter and adjust the consistency.

The driers – are those ingredients, which absorb the excess moisture in the batter and include flour, milk powder, and cocoa powder.

The problem in Balancing is that certain ingredients perform more than one function. Eggs provide toughening but are also a moistening agent. Milk is a moistening agent, but milk powder is a drier!!!! The aim of formula balancing is to balance the moisteners with the driers and the tougheners with the softeners. A simple sponge recipe may be in perfect balance, but when converted into a chocolate cake, the addition of cocoa powder in the recipe will mean additional driers so the corresponding moistening (addition of milk) will have to be increased as well.

There are three simple rules that govern Formula Balancing:

- The weight of the fat should not exceed the egg.
- The weight of the fat should not exceed the sugar
- The weight of the sugar should not exceed the total liquid

The Effect of Sugar: Sugar sweetens. It also has the power to lift and lighten the cake and to give the crust its color. It improves the taste and the flavour of the cake as well as the keeping quality and it adds to its nutritive value. The extra sugar in a recipe will result in the M Fault, when the extra sugar has lifted the batter to such an extent that the protein – starch structure can no longer hold up the cake and collapses. Excess sugar will result in spots on the crust and the crumb will be sticky (excess moisture). On the other hand, if the batter is made with less sugar, it will have a decreased volume with a peaked surface. The crumb will be dry and harsh. The peaked top is the result of the lack of softening action of the sugar on the gluten, which in turn will have greater resistance to expansion resulting in a peaked top.

The Effect of Fat: Fat imparts a rich and pleasant eating quality to the cake and increases the food value. Butter adds flavor and improves the quality of the cake. Because of its shortening property, fat/butter also prevents toughness. It holds the air that is incorporated in the initial process of creaming. Too much fat in a recipe will result in a cake of poor vol; Ume. The top crust will be thick and greasy. An increase in fat must be balanced by an increase in the toughners (structural material) like flour and egg. Less fat will make the cake tough, the volume will be poor and the crumb structure will show tunnel like holes pointing to the centre of the crown of the cake.

The Effect of Baking Powder: Baking Powder is used for aeration, thus increasing the volume of the cake. Some recipes do not use baking powder and the aeration is provided by mechanical means like creaming or beating (of eggs) or by sieving. Excess baking powder will produce the same effect as an excess of sugar will produce. The only difference is that there is a generation of gas beyond that which the flour and egg can take, with the result, the cake collapses. The crust of the cake is darker than normal and the crumb is open and is discolored especially near the base of the cake. Less baking powder will produce a cake of poor volume.

Characteristics of cakes:

1. **Volume:** It is difficult to set standards for volume of cakes which will vary according to different types of cakes and also according to consumer preference. However, the cakes should not have a pinched appearance and should not appear over extended too. A well risen cake will have a pleasing appearance with slight convex top surface. Although, the relative weight of a particular volume of cake will differ in different types of cakes, but a cake should not appear too small or too large for its weight.
2. **Colour of crust:** The crust should have a pleasing golden brown colour. Too dark or too light or dull colour is not desirable. Crust must have a uniform colour, free from dark streaks or sugar spots or grease spots.
3. **Symmetry of form:** Cakes should have a symmetrical appearance. Peaking, low sides, sunken or high centre, burst, caved in bottom or uneven top are undesirable characteristics of cakes.
4. **Character of crust:** Crust of a good cake should be thin and tender. Thick, rubbery, sticky or over moist, too tender, tough or blistery crust is indicative of poor quality of cakes

5. **Texture:** Texture denotes the pliability and smoothness of the crumb as felt by sense of touch. It depends on the physical condition of the crumb and type of grain. A good texture is soft and velvety without weakness and should not be crumby. Rough, harsh, too compact, lumpy or too loose texture is not desirable.

6. **Grain:** The grain is the structure formed by the extended gluten strands including the area they surrounded. Grain will vary according to the type of cake. However; uniformity of the size of cell and thin cell walls are desirable qualities. Coarseness, thick cell walls, uneven size of cells, large holes and tunnels are indicative of poor grain. Grain should not be too open or too close.

7. **Colour of crumb:** Crumb should have a lively, lustrous and uniform colour. It should be free from any streaks or dark patches. Grey, non – uniform, dark, light or dull colour of crumb will be undesirable.

8. **Aroma:** Aroma of good cake should be pleasant, rich, sweet and natural. It is not desirable to have any foreign aroma i.e. aroma not produced by normal ingredients of cake. Flat, musty, strong or sharp aroma is indicative of poor quality of cake.

9. **Taste:** Taste of a cake should be pleasant, sweet and satisfying. Cakes should not have any unpleasant after taste in the mouth, should not have a blend taste and should not have any foreign taste i.e. taste which cannot be acquired by the use of normal ingredients of cakes. Use of excessive salt or soda will also adversely affect the taste.

CHAPTER TWENTY

SPECIALITY CAKES

The term specialty cake is generally used to describe a cake that has been filled, iced, and has some type of finishing touch on the icing. Whether or not the cake is decorated attractively can influence your sales to a great degree. The decoration should tempt the customer to try the product and, at the same time, it should suggest the flavor and texture of the cake and filling. The decoration is the final wrapping, or packaging, designed to market your product.

Wedding and specialty cakes are a culmination of the talent, skills, and knowledge of the pastry chef or baker. To make a beautiful and flavorful cake, the pastry chef or baker must hone his or her skills in almost all aspects of the baking and pastry arts. Creation and development of cakes such as the ones in this chapter are limited only by the creativity of the individual.

Traditional British style wedding cakes are perhaps the quintessential wedding cakes, from which most other wedding cake styles are derived. These are, in general, unfilled dark fruitcakes. The richness of the cake reflects a time when refrigeration was unavailable. Dried fruit, sugar, suet, and thick layers of coatings and icings helped the cakes stay fresh for one year, as the top layer would be saved and eaten on the couple's first anniversary. The cakes are traditionally coated with a layer of jam, then with marzipan, and finally with several coats of royal icing. The jam and marzipan keep the white icing from absorbing oils or moisture from the cake, while protecting the cake itself from moisture loss and staling. Traditional British –style cakes consist of three tiers supported by pillars, generally pastillage, and both the icing and the decoration, which consists of royal icing piping and pastillage, are pure white. The British cultural influence is reflected in the styles of wedding cakes that evolved in countries colonized by Britain. Decoration consists of minute royal icing piping and gum paste flowers. Colors, if used at all, are the softest of pastels. Although these cakes may be quite ornate, their overall appearance is very soft and delicate. The tiers may simply be stacked, may be supported on pillars, or, often, may be displayed on offset asymmetrical cake stands. Beautiful realistic flowers are created from gum paste, and royal icing embroidery, string work, flood work, and ornaments are used to create stunning and intricate effects.

The British cake also spawned American –style cakes. American wedding cakes are most clearly defined by the use of buttercream icing, buttercream piping décor, and buttercream roses, often colored. There is no single cake type of choice in American cakes, but pound cakes, high –ratio cakes, génoise, and carrot cakes are most common.

Modern wedding cake: *Modern style cakes* are efficient in production, visual and taste appeal and can be tailored to the customers liking. Simple elegance and a light, fresh appearance are the objectives, in contrast to the baroque ornamentation of more traditional styles. Cutouts can be made in advance, and then placed on the cake relatively quickly for decoration. The taste of the finished product is an important factor in favor of the modern – style wedding cake, with virtually no restrictions on the type of cake or fillings. Generally, as with modern cuisine, fresh and seasonal products are employed to their best advantage. If a customer loves fresh strawberry charlotte, there is no reason the patisserie cannot create a festive, attractive wedding cake composed of charlottes.

Speciality cakes: Specialty cakes employ many of the same techniques as do wedding cakes. There are two elements that distinguish wedding cakes from specialty cakes: Specialty cakes are typically not tiered or stacked as are wedding cakes, and they are most often less ornately decorated. In some respects, however, the creation of a specialty cake presents fewer restrictions for the pastry chef or baker's creativity. Specialty cakes are less limited by shape, color, and type of décor.

Types of décor for these cakes will be restricted only by ambient temperature and humidity.

CHAPTER TWENTY-ONE

CAKE FAULTS

Faults during post production of cake during icing and decoration of creamed and whipped cakes:

Icing and creaming, and decoration or garnishing are the last steps of cake making. Most of the cakes are decorated with creamed icing (butter cream and whipped cream) and now a day's icing with fondants is also becoming fashion. In the fondant icing, many designs and themes can be given. The use of moulds and stencil is required sometimes to give accuracy, variety and attractiveness with the desired finish.

Some of the common and major problems may be:

Curdling or breaking: This fault may arise during the production of icing for the cakes. As we know that, there are various types of icing like butter cream, fondant, whipped cream, meringue icing. So while prepare these icing there may be chances of curdling which results in the uneven texture and may ruin your all efforts made for icing the cake. An utmost care must be taken while preparing and applying these types of icing over the cake so that even finishing and shine may be retained. Some remedies can be useful for such faults:

- Maintaining adequate temperature during production of icing especially for butter cream and whipping creaming. Preferably air-conditioned temperature is advised to get the better results.
- While whisking whipped or double cream, a bowl of ice can be placed under the whisking bowl.
- Remove water droplets, acidic particle or dirt if any in the bowl which may curdle the cream.
- Whip the cream slowly and in a controlled way.
- Don't over-whip – Once it just reaches stiff peaks, and then stop. Over- whipped cream will first turn grainy and then to butter or curdled.
- Use specific guideline given by the manufacturer of cream or such commodities.
- Same care must be taken while applying on the cakes; cake should be leveled and smoothened.
- Cakes must be moistened before applying the creams otherwise grainy particle may ruin the finishing.
- Cream should be taken in batches while adding colours and flavours and it should be used immediately otherwise after keeping for long time, cream may loose its texture or it may curdle.
- While making the meringue, the mixture should not be too hot when the butter is added.

Too Lumpy: This fault may arise due to adding sugar or other ingredient to the butter cream or other icing. If the sugar is not added properly to butter while creaming it may give lumpy texture to the cakes. Such problem may also happen in the fondant iced cake, where fondant may be exposed to air and may results into lumps while applying.

Some remedies for such fault may be:

- For the butter icing, super fine sugar should be used and it should be sifted two-three times before using to remove lumps if any.
- Fondant should be kept wrapped in cling film or plastic sheet to avoid craks or lumps.
- While rolling the fondant, there should be adequate temperature of the confectionery lab otherwise lumps or cracks may appear in the finished cake and may ruin all efforts.
- Make sure you sift all the dry ingredients separately before adding the liquid. Also, use only softened fats and add the sugar syrup very carefully.

Too stiff: sometimes cake may appear too stiff. This could be because of too stiff icing is applied on the cake. The most common reason for this is that the liquid content is too less, or that the icing is too cold. Remedy for such fault:

- Adjust the formula, something that can only be perfected with practice.
- In the case of the icing being too cold, wait until it reaches room temperature. You can even heat it slightly if required.

Not Adhering/Too Thin: if you have observed, sometimes we apply the icing hurriely on a slightly warm or hot cakes, icing (cream or butter) swirls down and give an effect of thin or not adhering icing. This may sometime happen due to thin icing or improper whisked cream. Some remedy for such fault may be:

- Always be patient and wait until cake reaches the room temperature.
- When the icing seems thin, you just need to wait for it to cool down. It usually ends up becoming a lot thicker.
- Follow the right technique for application.

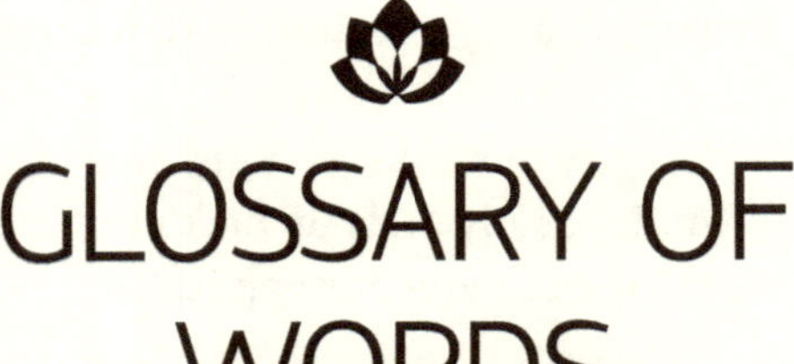

CHAPTER TWENTY-TWO

GLOSSARY OF WORDS

1. **Anpan** – A bun that is filled, usually with red bean paste, or with white beans, sesame, or chestnut

2. **Bakpao** – Indonesian term for steamed bun. The bun is usually filled with pork, but can also be filled with other ingredients, such as chicken, peanuts, or mung beans.

3. **Bánh bao** – Vietnamese meaning "Enveloping Cake", which is a ball –shaped bun containing pork or chicken meat, onions, eggs, mushrooms and vegetables, in the Vietnamese cuisine

4. **Baozi** – A type of steamed, filled bun or bread –like item made with baker's yeast in various Chinese cuisines, as there is much variation as to the fillings and the preparations

5. **Blaa** – A dough –like, white bread bun (roll) speciality particularly associated with Waterford, Ireland; historically, the blaa is also believed to have been made in Kilkenny and Wexford.

6. **Black treacle** – This is often used in rich fruit cakes and other full –flavoured bakes.

7. Bread roll – A short, oblong, or round bun served usually before or with meals, often with butter.

8. **Breakfast roll** – The breakfast roll is a bread roll filled with elements of a traditional fried breakfast. It typically consists of a bread roll or baguette containing one or more fillings such as sausages, bacon, white or black pudding, butter, mushrooms, tomatoes and tomato sauce or brown sauce. In some cases a hash brown, baked beans or fried egg may be added.

9. **Bun** – A bun is a small, sometimes sweet, bread –based roll. Though they come in many shapes and sizes, they are most commonly hand –sized or smaller, with a round top and flat bottom. Buns are usually made from flour, sugar, milk, yeast and butter. Common sweet varieties contain small fruit or nuts, and may topped with icing or caramel, or filled with jam or cream. Some types of buns are filled with various meats, or used to serve meats (such as hotdogs or hamburgers).

10. **Bunuelo** — A fried dough ball popular in Latin America, Greece, Guam, Turkey, Israel and Morocco. It will usually have a filling or a topping.

11. **Candied peel** – Made from sugared citrus fruits, candied peel is frequently used in Christmas cakes, panettone and Florentine biscuits.

12. **Challah Roll** – is a special bread in Jewish cuisine, usually braided and typically eaten on ceremonial occasions such as Shabbat and major Jewish holidays (other than Passover).

13. **Cheese bun** – A variety of small, baked, cheese –flavored rolls, a popular snack and breakfast food in Bolivia, Brazil (especially in the state of Minas Gerais), Paraguay, Colombia and northern Argentina.

14. **Chelsea bun** – A currant bun that is first created in the 18th century at the Chelsea Bun House in Chelsea, London, an establishment favoured by Hanoverian royalty which was demolished in 1839.

15. **Cinnamon bun** – A sweet roll served commonly in Northern Europe and North America; its main ingredients are dough, cinnamon, sugar, and butter, which provide a robust and sweet flavor

16. **Cocktail bun** – A Hong Kong –style sweet bun with a filling of shredded coconut; one of several iconic types of baked goods originating from Hong Kong.

17. **Concha** – are known for their shell –like shape and sugar shell pattern on the top. It is similar to Japanese melon pan. This is one of the most famous Mexican pastries and widely recognized in the United States. It is also referred to as "pan de huevo" (egg bread) in other Latin American countries, such as Chile, where they are eaten during tea time or at the beach.They are known as Cemitas in Honduras.

18. **Cream bun** – A bun that varies all around the world; typically they are made with an enriched dough bread roll that is baked and cooled, then split and filled with cream.

19. **Curry bread** – Some Japanese curry is wrapped in a piece of dough, which is coated in flaky bread crumbs, and usually deep fried or baked.

20. **Dampfnudel** – A white bread roll or sweet roll eaten as a meal or as a dessert in Germany and in France (Alsace); a typical dish in southern Germany.

21. **Desiccated coconut** – If you like coconut –flavoured cakes or cakes spread with jam and dipped in coconut then keep a packet of unsweetened desiccated coconut to hand.

22. **Dried fruit** – If you're a fruit cake fan, it's good to have a bag of currants, sultanas and raisins in the cupboard. There are plenty of other dried fruits available so buy them as you need them or select your favorites to modify a recipe.

23. **Food Colours** – This is an important constituent of cake as every cake is associated with a certain type of colour. Addition of colour it gives the food an attractive and appetizing appearance. Dyes of various colours (most commonly blue, green, red and yellow) are used to the cakes. Food colorings are available in small to big bottles in liquid form and in wide variety of colors.

24. **French roll** – a circular or oval bread roll having a hard or crispy crust. Also called French twist. Named after a coiffure for women in which the hair is combed back from the face and arranged in a vertical roll on the back of the head.

25. **Fruit bun** – A sweet roll made with fruit, fruit peel, spices and sometimes nuts; a tradition in Britain and former British colonies including Jamaica, Australia, Singapore, and India.

26. **Glacé cherries** –You can buy either the bright red glacé cherries which are dyed or the deeper red un –dyed cherries for use in fruit cakes, particularly Christmas cake.

27. **Golden syrup** – Sticky and sweet, golden syrup makes a moist sticky cake and, like black treacle, keeps for a long time in the cupboard.

28. **Ground almonds** – Ground almonds are often used in place of flour or as well as flour in cake recipes. They produce a moist cake and are suitable as a gluten –free option.

29. **Hamburger bun** – A round bun designed to encase a hamburger; invented in 1916 by a fry cook named Walter Anderson, who co –founded White Castle in 1992.

30. **Honey** – Honey is often used in addition to sugar and creates a moist and fragrant cake.

31. **Hot cross bun** – A sweet, spiced bun usually made with fruit but with other varieties such as apple –cinnamon or maple syrup and blueberries and marked with a cross on the top, traditionally eaten on Good Friday in the UK, Australia, New Zealand, South Africa, and Canada, but now popular all year round.

32. **Hot dog bun** – A long, soft bun shaped specifically to contain a hot dog or frankfurter.

33. **Jam** –Smooth apricot jam is a must if you like to make celebration cakes as it's used to stick marzipan on to fruit cake. Strawberry or raspberry jams are also good as a filling for a Victoria sandwich.

34. **Lemons, limes, oranges** – A little bit of zest can liven up a plain sponge mix. Some recipes also require the juice to make a sugar syrup for drizzling.

35. **Mandarin roll** – A steamed bun originating from China; cooked by steaming; a food staple of Chinese cuisine which is similar to white bread in western cuisine.

36. **Nuts** – Mixed chopped nuts, walnut halves, hazelnuts, flaked almonds and pecans are among the nuts you might want to have on hand. Again, choose the ones you like the best. Often one type of nut can be substituted for another in recipes. Store nuts in airtight containers as they might get rancid in contact to air.

37. **Parker House roll** – s a bread roll made by flattening the center of a ball of dough with a rolling pin so that it becomes an oval shape and then folding the oval in

half. They are made with milk and are generally quite buttery, soft, and slightly sweet with a crispy shell. They were invented at the Parker House Hotel in Boston, during the 1870s.

38. **Pâte à foncer** is French shortcrust pastry that includes egg. Egg and butter are worked together with a small quantity of sugar and salt before the flour is drawn into the mixture and cold water added to bind it.

39. **Pâte brisée** is similar to pâte à foncer, but is lighter and more delicate due to an increased quantity of butter – up to three –fifths the quantity of flour. Very often is made with no sugar, as a savoury crust for pies.

40. **Pâte sablée** has the same ingredients as pâte sucrée, but the butter is creamed with the sugar and the eggs before the flour is folded in. This mixes the butter more evenly, which makes the dough puff much less, creating a more "snappy" and dry pastry, instead of the crumbly texture of the previous doughs. Sablée works better for sweet tarts, tea biscuits, and piped shapes than other short doughs, as they hold their shape much more efficiently, and are the basis for gingerbread and sandwich biscuits. No water is needed, neither is the dough particularly temperature –sensitive

41. **Pâte sucrée** (sweetcrust pastry, sweet dough, or sweet paste) is made with more sugar, which sweetens the mix and impedes the gluten strands, creating a pastry that breaks up easily in the mouth. An alternative is gluten –free pastry.

42. **Piggy bun** – A Hong Kong pastry that is essentially the equivalent of the French baguette; found in Hong Kong bakeries and Cha chaan teng; in Hong Kong, it is often cut in half and served with butter and condensed milk.

43. **Polenta** – Polenta is another flour substitute – cakes made with this ingredient tend to be denser, pleasantly textured and have a vibrant yellow colour.

44. **Pork chop bun** – famous and popular snack in Macau, the "piggy bun" is crisp outside and soft inside; a freshly fried pork chop is filled into it

45. **Ritually** –acceptable challah is made of dough from which a small portion has been set aside as an offering.

46. **Rum roll** – historic Washington D.C. specialty, similar to a cinnamon bun with rum flavored icing.

47. **Sally Lunn bun** – A enriched yeast bread associated with the city of Bath in the West Country of England.

48. **Semla** – A traditional sweet roll made in various forms in Denmark, the Faroe Islands, Iceland, Estonia, Finland, Latvia, Lithuania, Sweden and Norway; associated with Lent and especially Shrove Monday and Shrove Tuesday; the oldest version of the semla was a plain bread bun, eaten in a bowl of warm milk; in Swedish this is known as Hetvägg

49. **Shengjian mantou** – A type of small, pan –fried baozi which is a specialty of Shanghai and usually filled with pork and gelatin that melts into soup/liquid when cooked.

50. **Siopao** – Hokkien term for baozi, literally meaning "steamed buns"; it has also been incorporated into Thai cuisine where it is called salapao.

51. **Sticky bun** – A dessert or breakfast sweet roll that generally consists of rolled pieces of leavened dough, sometimes containing brown sugar or cinnamon, which are then compressed together to form a flat loaf corresponding to the size of the baking pan; they have been consumed since the Middle Ages, at which time cinnamon became more prominent.

52. **Sufganiyah** – A deep –fried bun, filled with jam or custard, and then topped with powdered sugar. Typically eaten in Israel during Hanukkah.

53. **Sunflower oil** – Sunflower oil has many culinary uses and it's ideal for baking as it has a mild flavour which allows the other ingredients in a cake to shine through.

54. **Sweet roll** – A sweet roll or sweet bun refers to any of a number of sweet, baked, yeast – leavened breakfast or dessert foods. They may contain spices, nuts, candied fruits, etc., and are often glazed or topped with icing. Compared to regular bread dough, sweet roll dough generally has higher levels of sugar, fat, eggs, and yeast. They are often round, and are small enough to comprise a single serving.

55. **Teacake** – A fruited sweet bun usually served toasted and buttered.

56. **Tingmo** – Steamed bread in Tibetan cuisine. It is sometimes described as a steamed bun that is similar to Chinese flower rolls. It does not contain any kind of filling.

57. **Xiaolongbao** – A steamed bun from the Jiangnan region of China; fillings vary by region and usually include some meat and/or a gelatin –gelled aspic that becomes a soup when steamed.

58. **Zeeuwse bolus** – A spiral shaped bun covered in dark brown sugar, lemon zest and cinnamon.

CHAPTER TWENTY-THREE

Summary:

Dough is a thick, malleable, sometimes elastic paste made out of any grains, leguminous or chestnut crops. Dough is typically made by mixing flour with a small amount of water and/or other liquid, and sometimes includes yeast or other leavening agents as well as other ingredients such as various fats or flavorings.

Basic sweet yeast dough is enriched dough, also known as rich dough. This means that the dough is made with fat, sugar, and sometimes eggs, as opposed to lean doughs that do not have any fat present. The addition of fat to yeast dough creates bread that tends to have a softer crust and less chewy crumb and is more flavorful in general.

A Danish pastry, sometimes also known as just Danish, is a multilayered, laminated sweet pastry in the viennoiserie tradition. This pastry type is named Danish because it originates from Denmark. The concept was brought to Denmark by Austrian bakers, and has since developed into a Danish specialty. Like other Viennoiserie pastries, such as croissants, it is a variant of puff pastry made of laminated yeast –leavened dough that creates a layered texture. It consists out of yeast –leavened dough and a type of fat; mostly butter or margarine.

Croissants are a style of crescent shaped Viennoiserie pastries of Austria.Viennoiseries in French comes from the word "Viennois" for people and things from Vienna. The legend takes place during the Ottoman Turk siege of the city; a baker apparently heard the Turks tunneling under the walls of the city as he lit his ovens to bake the morning bread. He quickly sounded an alarm, and the military collapsed the tunnel, saving the city. To celebrate, the baker baked crescent –shaped bread'kipferl', in the shape of the crescent moon of the Turkish flag.

A roll cake is a cake that is rolled. A roll cake is often called a Swiss roll, jelly roll, roll cake, cream roll, or Swiss log. It's a type of sponge cake that is filled with whipped cream, jam or frosting and then rolled into a spiral before serving. A roll cake is similar to a roulade but a roulade can be filled with other things besides sweet fillings and can even be savory. The origins of the term are unclear. In spite of the name "Swiss roll", the cake is believed to have originated in the nineteenth century elsewhere in Central Europe, likely Austria.

A bun is a small, sometimes sweet, bread –based item or roll. Though they come in many shapes and sizes, they are most commonly hand –sized or smaller, with a round top and flat bottom. Buns are usually made from flour, sugar, milk, yeast, butter and occasionally egg. Common sweet varieties contain small fruit or nuts, and may topped with icing or caramel, or filled with jam or cream. Some types of buns are filled with various meats, or used to serve meats (such as hotdogs or hamburgers). "Bun" may also refer to particular types of filled dumplings, such as Chinese *baozi*. Some of these types of dumplings may be bread –like in texture. They are also called Dinner roll in England.

Doughnuts are deep –fried round wheel or ring shaped cakes or confectionary with a hole and with roots in European history in the Middle Eastern cuisine. They were introduced to America by the Dutch as *oliekoecken* (oil cakes or fried cakes). Another history illustrates that in ancient Rome and Greece, cooks would fry strips of pastry dough and coat them with honey or fish sauce. In Medieval times, Arab cooks started frying up small portions of unsweetened yeast dough, drenching the plain fried blobs in sugary syrup to sweeten them. These Arab fritters spread into northern Europe in the 1400's and became very popular Europe. Doughnuts are made of yeast dough rich in eggs and butter, spices and dried fruits, their sweetness came from the fruit and the final dusting of sugar.

Crullers are rich, light disk or oblong shaped cakes, similar to doughnuts, but are made of rich dough twisted or curled, fried in deep fat and topped with white icing. Crullers are most commonly found in Canada, New England, the Mid –Atlantic and North Central states of the United States, but are also common in California. The German origin is probably why traditional crullers can be found more easily in the Midwest, where many German immigrants settled.

Short crust pastry is the simplest and most common pastry. It is made with flour, fat, butter, salt, sugar, water and sometimes egg and milk to bind the dough. This is used mainly in preparation of tarts, quiche or pie, biscuits and cookies. The flour should have low gluten content, one that is milled from soft wheat flour. The fat will reduce the extensibility of the gluten that is it makes the gluten strands shorter, hence the term *shortening* for the fat used in the bakery and the term *short crust pastry*.

Puff pastry is one of the most remarkable products of the bakeshop. Although it includes no added leavening agent, it can rise to eight times its original thickness when baked. Puff pastry is rolled –in dough, like Danish and croissant doughs. This means that it is made up of many layers of fat sandwiched between layers of dough. Puff pastry can be made as upto thousand layers or more. The whole purpose of rolling and folding is to build up a layered structure of alternating layers of dough and fat. This process is known as *lamination*.

An éclair is an oblong pastry made with choux dough filled with a pastry cream or custard and topped with chocolate icing or dipped in fondant icing. The word comes from the French éclair, meaning "flash of lightning", so named because it is eaten quickly (in a flash).The dough, which is the same as that used for profiterole, is typically piped into an oblong shape with a pastry bag and baked until it is crisp and hollow inside. A cream puff (US), profiterole (English) or chou à la crème (French) is a filled French choux pastry ball with a typically sweet and moist filling of whipped cream, custard, pastry cream, or ice cream. The puffs may be decorated or left plain or garnished with chocolate sauce, caramel, or a dusting of powdered sugar.

Cream cheese is an American invention developed in 1872 in New York State. It is a soft cow's –milk, mild tangy tasting fresh cheese with a high fat content (approx 35%), spreadable texture and creamy white in colour. Cream cheese is categorized as a fresh cheese since it is unaged. As a result, it has a short shelf life, once opened. It is available in various sized solid white blocks or whipped and flavored. Cream cheese should be gently softened before blending them into fillings, icings and batters. Blend the cheese on low speed with a paddle to soften and remove lumps before adding sugar, eggs or other liquid ingredient.

Icing, also known as frosting, is a sweet decorative creamy glaze coating used as a filling between the layers or as a coating over the top and sides of a cake. It is used to add flavor and to improve a cake's appearance. Icing can also extend a cake's shelf life by forming a protective coating. There are seven general types of icing: butter cream, foam, fudge, fondant, glaze, royal icing and ganache. Each type can be produced with a number of formulas and in a range of flavorings. Because icing is integral to the flavor and appearance of many cakes, it should be made carefully using high –quality ingredients and natural flavors and colors. A good icing is smooth; it is never grainy or lumpy. It should complement the flavor and texture of the cake without overpowering it. A basic icing is called a glacé, containing powdered sugar (also known as icing sugar or confectioners' sugar) and water.

Cakes have their part to play in ancient beliefs and superstitions, some which still carries on to modern times. In olden times, people used cakes as offerings to their gods and spirits around the world. The Chinese celebrate Harvest Moon festival and have moon cakes to honour their moon goddess. This tradition continues up to today. Russians have sun cakes called blini which are thin pancakes to pay their respect to a deity called Maslenitsa.

There are many different types of cakes and many different ways of dividing them into various categories, but professional bakers categorize cakes by ingredients and mixing method. (Home bakers tend to categorize cakes by flavoring –i.e., chocolate cakes, fruit cakes, and so on –which is helpful when you're trying to decide what to eat, but not as helpful when you're trying to understand how best to make a cake.) Depending on how the batter is prepared, you will find that the final texture (and color, if it is a yellow or white cake) varies.

Cake Improvers are "miracle ingredient." When added to cake batter at the creaming stage, it supposedly renders the crumb soft and moist and increases shelf life. The mysterious product contains rice starch, polyglycerol esters, and mono – and di –glycerides – the same additives found in many boxed cake mixes and commercial baked goods.

A cake formula is an accurate record of the quantities of the raw materials necessary to make a particular type of cake. If the recipe is correct, it will produce a good cake. As important as the recipe is the correct temperature, time and packing of the product. A good cake is one showing no faults, either in appearance, texture or while eating. It should be of good flavor and aroma and if it contains fruits, they must be evenly distributed. Bakery being the science that it is, we refer to the recipe as a formula. In the bakery, the range of ingredients that are used and which are essential is limited. There is Flour, Fat, Sweetening and Moistening. Each of these has a specific role to play and must be in Balance with each other.

The Author

Dr. Anshumali Pandey is a renowned & reliable name in the field of Education, Hospitality, Tourism and Tribal Food. He is a Teacher and Chef by profession, and also an Author, a Business Auditor, and an avid culinary traveller to the Indian Sub continental hinterlands. Dr. Anshumali Pandey is a Hospitality Educator (PhD) who specialises in Higher Education, Office Administration, Pay roll, HR, Labour Laws, Audit, and Procurement & Tender Process. He is an Author with 80 Publications consisting of 62 Books and 3 short stories.

His contribution and research in the field of Tribal Food, Tribal Tourism, Forest Tourism and Village Tourism in the form of research papers have brought several laurels to him. In 2018 the Ministry of Tourism, Govt of Indian duly recognised all this and awarded him with a National Appreciation certificate and memento.

The books written by **Dr Anshumali Pandey** are essentially a banquet arising from an experience of over 26 years of Professional life and have boiled down to crisp and accurate writing on his favourite subjects. Hospitality Sector champion requires to be a specialist in many fields and Dr Pandey is one of them. His knowledge is evident from the spectrum of subjects which he has chosen for his books so far, which ranges from being a specialist chef, to Master of Human resources, to Education and to love for children, and topped with Spirituality. For more than two decades Dr Pandey has lived with his family in Western India in general and the Tribal belt of the union territory of Dadra & Nagar Haveli in particular. Most of his time is consumed in helping and understanding the Tribal and rural population of the region and writing scholarly articles and books on his vast area of interest.

Books written by the Author are –

1. Theory of Indian Cookery
2. Beauty and Irony of Silvassa Tourism
3. A Short Indian Food Story
4. Be Your Own Guide to Indian Cuisine
5. Cookery Fundamentals
6. History of Indian Food (2 Editions Printed)
7. The Great Indian Story Book for Children
8. Personal Budget: Easy Work Book
9. Online Classes Log Book
10. Dictionary Making Work Book for School Children
11. The Lazy Bed
12. Hindu Dharm (हिन्दू धर्म) (In Hindi Language)
13. Where is my coffee?
14. Your First Job is Never your Last (Volume 1)

15. You are Almost There (Quick Fix Resume and Interview Hacks)
16. Working for the Enemy? - A lesson in Career Management
17. Public Speaking for the Young
18. A Date With Coffee
19. How to be The Best Hotel Front Office Employee
20. Diploma in Food Production, The complete Syllabus
21. Diploma in F&B Service, The Complete Syllabus
22. Diploma in Front Office, The Complete Syllabus
23. The Time to Speak is Now
24. Munshi Premchand (Short Stories in English)
25. The Housekeeping Department, Text Book
26. Hitchhiker's Guide to Trekking in Uttarakhand
27. Uttarakhand, A divine Land for a Reason
28. Bachhon ke liye rochak kahaniyan (बच्चों के लिए रोचक कहानियाँ) (In Hindi Language)
29. Basic Communication Skills of English
30. The Basic Office Organisation Book for Start-ups
31. Hospitality HRM
32. Hospitality Marketing
33. Bakery Ingredients and Tools
34. Human Resource Management for Indian Professionals
35. The process of LAWFULLY operating a Hospitality business in India
36. Indian Classical Sweets: History, Tradition and Recipes
37. History of India's Himalayan Cuisine: Classical Cookery of Kashmir, Laddakh, Jammu, Himachal, Lahaul, Spiti, Garhwal, Kumaon.
38. Vindu: Andhra Cuisine (Part 1 of South Indian Trilogy)
39. Saappadu: Tamil Cuisine (Part 2 of South Indian Trilogy)

40. Sadya: Malayali Cuisine (Part 3 of South Indian Trilogy)
41. South Indian Cuisine - The Researcher's Guide Book
42. The Ramayana for Children and other short stories from Indian Mythology
43. Legends of the Tribal Shiva
44. Third Generation Children's Story Book
45. It's Elementary: The Top Nine Adventures from the memoirs of Dr John H Watson
46. UNITY IN DIVERSITY, The foundation of Indian Tourism
47. The Thar Express: Culinary History of Rajasthan and Gujarat
48. Basics of Computerized Accounting
49. Impact (Impact of Globalization on Indian Social Life)
50. Vishnu – The Lord of Amazing Incarnations
51. Being a Mahatma in the Freedom Struggle
52. The Culinary Journey of Purvanchal: Lucknow to Patna
53. Culinary History of the Gangetic Plains
54. Indian Culinary Secrets
55. The Story of Jain and Parsi Food
56. The Great Indian Pilgrimage Tourism
57. Introduction to Tourism Studies – Text Book
58. Bread and Rolls
59. Diploma in Digital Marketing the Complete Syllabus
60. **The Theory of Sweetened Bakery Foods**
61. Campus Placement Guide for Management Trainee in Leading Hotels
62. Diploma in Housekeeping Management, the Complete Syllabus

Connect with me: anshumali.pandey@gmail.com
https://notionpress.com/author/337004

Please scan this QR code on your phone to know more about the latest and complete works of Dr Anshumali Pandey